The
Carousel Keepers

The Carousel Keepers

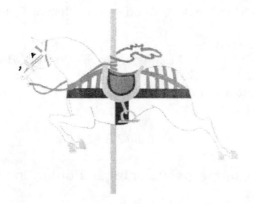

An Oral History
of
American Carousels

by

Carrie Papa

The McDonald & Woodward Publishing Company
Blacksburg, Virginia
1998

The McDonald & Woodward Publishing Company
Blacksburg, Virginia 24060

The Carousel Keepers: An Oral History of American Carousels

© 1998 by The McDonald & Woodward Publishing Company

Composition by Rowan Mountain, Inc., Blacksburg, Virginia
Printed in the United States of America by
McNaughton & Gunn, Inc., Saline, Michigan
First printing July 1998

06 05 04 03 02   10 9 8 7 6 5 4 3 2

Library of Congress Cataloging in Publication Data

Papa, Carrie, 1926–
    The carousel keepers : an oral history of American carou-
sels / by Carrie Papa.
        p.   cm.
    Includes bibliographical references (p.) and index.
    ISBN 0-939923-67-X (alk. paper)
    1. Merry-go-round—United States—History. 2. Amuse-
ment parks—United States—
    Employees—Interviews.   I. Title.
    GV 1860.M4P36   1994
    796'.06'8—dc21

                                                    96-48713
                                                    CIP

Contents

Acknowledgements

Sincere appreciation is extended to the New Jersey Historical Commission for a local history grant, which made possible
the Carousel Keepers Oral History Project. Love and gratitude
is offered to Albert for his support and patience during the
months of interviewing, transcribing, editing, and writing of
this history and to Jo Anne for all of her suggestions and editing assistance. Thanks also to Alexis Kulick for help with the
computer.

Special thanks to Frank Messino, Melissa Hollister and the
Chemung County Historical Society, Ed Aswad and Carriage
House Photography, Karen Gilbert and the Newark Public Li-
brary, Charles Ridgeway and the Walt Disney World Company,
Beth McFarland and the City Park carousel, Louise DeMars and
the New England Carousel Museum, Susan Blakely and
Westlake Conservators, James Abbate and the National Amuse-
ment Park Historical Association, Daniel Satow and Norton
Auctioneers, Fern Ottomano, Christopher Scott and the Martha's
Vineyard Preservation Trust, Brunner Barrie and Sculpture
House, Inc., Six Flags Theme Parks, Alison Shaw, Karen Smith,
and Dr. Norma Menghetti for the use of their photographs.

I am grateful to Nellie and Joseph DeLorenzo, Martin Kane,
and Laurie Martin for additional information and photographs
of Bertrand Island Amusement Park and to Anthony Falcone
for information on the Casino Building in Asbury Park, New
Jersey.

I also want to thank my editor, Jerry McDonald, for all of
his help.

Finally, to those "Carousel Keepers," who so graciously
shared their memories and photographs with me, I offer a very
sincere thank you to each and every one: Sol Abrams; Randall
Bailey; Robert Bennett; Scott Bittler; Joseph Bornman; Jane

Chittick; Terry Cicalese; Raymond D'Agostino; Dennis Desjarlais; Charlotte Dinger; Gail Domin; William Finkenstein; William Foster; Kim Fraker; David Gillian; Roy Gillian; Toni Grekin; Joyce Hanks; Susan Hofsass; Gerry Holzman; Dell Hopson; Edward Lange; Jane P. R. Lee; George W. Long, Jr.; Mabel Long; Kenneth Lynch; John McIntosh; William Moore; Dr. Floyd Moreland; Merrick Price; Albert Reid; Bernd Rennebeck; Richard Schiess; Gary Swarer; Justin Van Vliet; Charles Walker; and Paul Woehle.

Introduction

In the early years of the twentieth century some six thousand hand-carved wood carousels were to be found in America. Today, fewer than two hundred operating antique merry-go-rounds remain. As recently as 1987, there were twenty-one working historic carousels in New Jersey. Today, only four are left and they are in jeopardy. Coinciding with the loss of the historic carousel, the amusement industry itself has undergone dramatic changes. The small family-owned-and-operated amusement park gave way during and after the 1950s to large corporate theme parks devoted to ever faster rides and action involvement. This development almost certainly contributed to the demise of the historic merry-go-round. Another factor contributing to the loss of complete carousels is the changed view of the carousel from an amusement attraction to an authentic art object. Contemporary interest in the hand-carved carousel figures as American folk sculpture resulted in many historic machines being broken up in order to sell the individual animals piece by piece. The carousel figure that a master carver was paid twenty dollars to make in the early years of the twentieth century now brings between $10,000 and $150,000.

Although the carousel dates back to the fifth century AD, it is still considered the "diamond" on the midway or the "centerpiece" of amusement and theme parks. As the National Carousel Association puts it, "carousels or merry-go-rounds are the most important part of the amusement business."[1] In fact, the carousel often was the forerunner of the amusement park. The merry-go-round was first popularized in America in picnic groves, town parks, and seaside resorts where late-nineteenth-century Americans gathered to relax and have fun. Eventually, as the industrial revolution progressed, many of the summer resorts evolved into full scale amusement parks designed to

Figure 1. "Cinderella's Golden Carousel" at the Magic Kingdom in Walt Disney World, Orlando, Florida, was built in 1917 by the Philadelphia Toboggan Company. The magnificent carousel was originally named "Liberty" as an expression of the patriotism that was prevalent during the First World War. (Photo: Walt Disney World Company)

Figure 2. Before Disney purchased PTC #46 in 1965, the carousel had been in operation at Olympic Park in Maplewood, New Jersey, for nearly forty years. (Photo: Walt Disney World Company)

entertain a growing middle-class that had more leisure time and money than ever before. But always the carousel remained the heart of the amusement park. While this is still true, it is regrettable that most of the carousels operating today are fiberglass replicas of antique merry-go-rounds that have been lost to the auctioneer's gavel. The hand-carved wooden carousel is fast disappearing from the American scene. At the rate that small amusement parks and their merry-go-rounds are becoming extinct, almost all of America's hand-carved carousels may be lost within another ten years. Also, as the people who were connected with these local parks and vintage machines pass from the scene, the social history that is part of our national carousel heritage goes with them.

Although several excellent books provide historical information on the master carvers and the early carousel companies, little has been recorded of the lives of the ordinary folk connected with carousels. Who were these people? What were their lives like? What were their problems? Their satisfactions? In 1989, The Carousel Keepers Oral History Project was designed to answer these questions by interviewing those most closely connected with New Jersey's amusement industry and taperecording their memories. The aim of the Project was to document the role of the carousel owner and the carousel itself in the setting of the amusement industry and the larger environment of the historical circumstances, conditions, and things that affected the carousel owner and his machine. As well as creating an archive of primary source material, the purpose of the Project was to increase the nearly non-existent body of knowledge about the lives of the people behind New Jersey's historic carousels, to make this history available to a broad audience, and to encourage the preservation of New Jersey's remaining carousels. To accomplish these goals, partial funding was obtained through a grant from the New Jersey Historical Commission, people involved with New Jersey carousels and amusement parks were located, and and an interview outline was prepared covering many topics. The following examples will give an idea of the type of questions asked during the interviews:

What kind of living did you make?

What were the satisfactions/problems in operating a carousel?

Was the carousel important to the community? Why?

What status did you have in the community?

What impact did national events (Great Depression, First and Second World Wars, boom times) have on you personally, on the carousel, on the amusement industry?

Were there government imposed restrictions or safety regulations?

Were there unions?

What skills were needed for running a carousel, maintenance, repairs, dealing with the public?

What was the social, ethnic, economic makeup of those visiting the carousel/amusement park?

Have the visitors changed through the years?

Any history of floods, fires, or other disasters?

To make the oral history collection available to other researchers and the public, interview transcripts were deposited with the Special Collections of the Alexander Library, Rutgers University, New Brunswick, New Jersey.

Articles utilizing the oral history collection were published in *New Jersey Folklife, The National Amusement Park Historical Association News, The Merry-go-roundup,* and *The Carousel News and Trader.* On the recommendation of the editors of these publications, the Project was expanded to include other nearby states. Narrators were then located in Massachusettes, New York, Connecticut, Pennsylvania, the District of Columbia, North Carolina, and Georgia.

The Carousel Keepers Oral History Project looked at the underlying culture, the intangible "way of life," that was part of our amusement heritage. In these first-hand accounts from the people behind America's merry-go-rounds, we see the "golden age" of the carousel through the eyes of the actual participants. This golden age stretched from the turn-of-the-century until the Second World War, which made materials and manpower scarce and further contributed to the decline of the small amusement park and the disappearance of the vintage carousels.

Thirty-seven individuals were interviewed for the Project. We now have a good historical record of where carousels and amusement parks fit into the leisure-time activities of Americans, how they influenced the economic development of par-

Figure 3. The dock entrance to Bertrand Island Amusement Park, a New Jersey Landmark since 1922. The park was torn down in 1983 to make room for condominiums. (Photo: From the collection of Ray D'Agostino)

ticular towns, and how they were viewed by local residents. Equally important, we now have the personal observations and memories of those who are part of this history. Through the pictures portrayed by these eye-witnesses, we gain a heightened sense of the times discussed. Through their memories, we step back in history to discover not only the romance of the grand old carousels, but we also learn of the long hours and hard work involved in running a merry-go-round. As we share their experiences, their successes and their failures, their joys, and their problems, we participate in the reality behind the nostalgia.

---

[1] Charles Walker, *The Carousel is the Greatest Show in Town,* Atlanta, GA: National Carousel Association, n.d.

The
Carousel Keepers

1

The Carousel Keepers

Those who recorded their memories for the oral history project range from George Long, Jr., carver of carousel figures and one time employee of the Philadelphia Toboggan Company to Dennis Desjarlais, who, in the tradition of the traveling carnival, was married on the merry-go-round at Seaside Heights, New Jersey. Owners of amusement parks, carvers of carousel animals, managers of a particular carousel, operators, electricians, workers, riders, and just plain folk all contributed their recollections of the past, their current involvement with merry-go-rounds, and their hopes for the carousel in the future. The narrators, with a brief introduction and an excerpt from the interview, are listed in alphabetical order. You will come to know these keepers of the carousels as they share their experiences and stories with you.

·⤳ Sol Abrams ⤳·

Sol Abrams served as Public Relations Director for Palisades Amusement Park in Cliffside, New Jersey, for more than thirty years. During his years as press agent for the wonderland on the Hudson, Mr. Abrams became legendary for his zany publicity stunts promoting Palisades. From putting an elephant on water skis in the Hudson River to the world's first Diaper Derby, Sol's publicity and wild ideas turned Palisades into one of the most famous amusement parks in America. His goal was to get

Figure 4. Sol Abrams and Eddie Fisher share a smile. (Photo: Courtesy Sol Abrams)

a story on Palisades in *Life Magazine* at least once a year. And his outrageous stunts did make *Life Magazine*, and newspapers, newsreels, radio, and television. Promotions like getting Eddie Fisher and Debbie Reynolds to announce their engagement on the stage at the park, or having Chubby Checker introduce the Twist there, featuring the Triplet's Convention or the Beautiful Legs Contest, not only brought publicity but also the crowds to Palisades Amusement Park. On the Eddie Fisher-Debbie Reynolds engagement, Sol reveals:

> Everybody would fight to get into *Life Magazine*. It was almost impossible. *Life* would shoot a thousand pictures for every one that they would use. On that Debbie Reynolds and Eddie Fisher engagement, there were mobs and mobs of kids, as far as you could see. So I wrote on the steps [of

the stage]: *Dearest Eddie, say it isn't so,* and I put the chalk in the hands of a teenage girl. To this day, they believe that one of the teenagers there wrote it. That picture appeared in *Life,* and the wire services and publications all over the world.

·⤳ Randall Bailey ⤳·

Randall Bailey is Assistant Manager of Park Operations of the theme park Six Flags Over Georgia. In his interview, Mr. Bailey explains the importance of having an original Philadelphia Toboggan Company carousel in the historically-themed park. Built in 1908, the carousel was originally installed in Riverview Park, Chicago. It was acquired by Six Flags Over Georgia in 1971 and installed in the Riverview Carousel building, which is styled after the original building in Chicago. Mr. Bailey was involved in the installation of Philadelphia Toboggan Company carousel #17 at Six Flags, and with great pride reported:

> To me, there's a something. . . . a magical mystique about the carousel. The horses are so incredibly beautiful and the colors are so vivid. Little kids always like vivid colors. Little kids and old people. It's the magic of that. The gleam in their eyes. They're so excited when they see it. I still get excited when I go up and see it. I'm proud of having been a part of it, seeing it when it was originally unloaded and a part of watching the whole restoration process. Then being on the first ride, the first time we ran it around. It's a very special feeling on my part.

·⤳ Robert Bennett ⤳·

In 1949, Robert Bennett started his career in the amusement industry operating rides and cleaning the swimming pool at Casino Pier in Seaside Heights, New Jersey. Today, he owns both the Casino Pier and the Waterworks in Seaside. The Casino Pier carousel also is known as the historic Floyd L. Moreland carousel. As with all of the respondents, Bob loves his work and enthusiastically stated:

> I don't ever want to retire. I love the business. I work very hard. In the summer months, I have to be here day and night, day and night. If it's eight in the morning till two in the morning, it doesn't make any difference. I'm here and I'm ready

to go. I get here at 8:30 in the morning, before we open. And I don't get out of here 'till 1:00 o'clock in the morning. Now I do that — I work seven days a week. I take Thursday nights off. Not Thursday day, but Thursday night. Even after forty years in the business, I still do this seven days a week. I love every minute of it.

·⤳ Scott Bittler ⤳·

Descendant of Edward Francis Long, patriarch of the Long family who built eight carousels, Robert Scott Bittler was named for his grandfather Robert A. Long, Jr. The Long family's involvement in the carousel business dates back to the late 1800s. In his interview, Mr. Bittler recalls his boyhood days of working with his grandfather, who began operating a merry-go-round at Eldridge Park, Elmira, New York, in 1924. After sixty-five years, the carousel, with its magnificent Carmel, Looff, and Dentzel animals was sold at auction in 1990. On the disappearance of the small family-run amusement park, Mr. Bittler laments:

> It saddens me because it's a piece of Americana that future generations just won't know of. It holds a lot of fond memories from my own upbringing that we won't be able to share with our kids.

·⤳ Joseph Bornman ⤳·

Manager and caretaker of the Sanitarium Playgrounds of New Jersey, Joseph Bornman tells about the history of the private philanthropic park and the underprivileged children they serve. The real treasure of the park is its Frederick Heyn carousel. Even though the horses need major restoration, Mr. Borman reports that this doesn't bother the children.

> Well, they need a lot of work, but the kids don't look at that, see. If you give a toy to a child and he's played with it for years and you go buy a new one, he looks at it, but likes that old one. Kids don't care about antiques. But what kid doesn't love a horse?

·⤳ Jane Chittick ⤳·

Jane Chittick, as Executive Director of the Martha's Vineyard Preservation Trust, was deeply involved in the purchase and preservation of the Society's Flying Horses. Carved by C. W. F. Dare, the nation's oldest platform carousel has been operating on the island of Martha's Vineyard since 1884. Although the carousel later was declared a National Historic Landmark, at the time the Society purchased the merry-go-round, Ms. Chittick reports that many members were opposed to the project.

> Some people thought that this was ridiculous for a preservation society. And what did we want with a merry-go-round? Others felt it was very important. The expense, $750,000 for a child's toy and a run-down one at that. Sort of a honky tonk amusement park, sort of a Coney Island thing. What will we do with it? What on earth does this have to do with historical preservation? So, it took convincing them.

·⤙ Terry Cicalese ⤚·

Terry Cicalese, employee of Jenkinson's Amusements in Point Pleasant, New Jersey, remembers from her childhood a beautiful, large merry-go-round at Point Pleasant and recalls:

> That carousel burned in a fire. Everybody got dressed up to come on to the boardwalk. [Today,] the dress code is completely changed. It just isn't the way it used to be. I see changes 'cause I live here, but I think it's the changes in people more than changes in the town. People just don't take care of things the way they did years ago.

·⤙ Raymond D'Agostino ⤚·

Owner of Bertrand Island Amusement Park on Lake Hopatcong, New Jersey, for thirty-five years, Raymond D'Agostino spent a lifetime in the amusement industry. Bertrand Island was demolished to make room for condominiums in 1978. In the early years, Mr. D'Agostino's father had concessions at Bertrand Island, but when the opportunity to buy the park came up, that's just what they did. In this section, Ray gives us a clue as to why housing at Lake Hopatcong might be a better investment than an amusement park today.

> Years ago when we first came up here, Lake Hopatcong was, I would say was seventy-five to eighty percent seasonal and twenty percent year round. It used to be when Labor Day came, most of the people would move back to the city

7

Figure 5. Ray D'Agostino spent a lifetime in the amusement industry. As a child, he helped his father operate their concession stands at Bertrand Island Amusement Park, Lake Hopatcong, New Jersey. In 1947, the D'Agostinos purchased the park and Ray managed it for the next thirty years. (Photo: Carrie Papa)

or wherever they came from, and the residency here dropped completely down. In the summertime, it would swell. You would get an additional seventy-five percent. But that all changed. In the last fifteen years or so, it is now less than five percent, I would say, of people that move away and ninety-five percent live here year round. I think the reason for that is that it probably became too expensive to maintain homes on the lake that are very expensive with taxes and everything else and try to have another home someplace else. So most of the people enjoyed it here so they decided to stay here year round. That's what happened.

·⌣ Dennis Desjarlais ⌣·

On May 10th, 1988, Dennis Desjarlais and his bride were married on the Floyd L. Moreland carousel in Seaside Heights, New Jersey. He tells us:

I came here from being on road carnivals and on road carnivals, they don't use any paper work. You just go to the merry-go-round with whoever you happen to choose as your spouse. You say your own vows and your friends all push you around once and you're married. Here, I went and got all the legal papers and so forth. Town Mayor, Seaside Heights Mayor married us. I've got a lot of sentimental feeling for that merry-go-round. We said our vows and then all of my friends that were there pushed it around once. Then everybody that was there at the ceremony got on and they took us for a ride.

·⤳ Charlotte Dinger ⤳·

Charlotte Dinger, author of *Art of the Carousel,* and owner of one of the finest collections of carousel art in the world, is an internationally recognized authority on carousels. Mrs. Dinger began her collection of carousel art in 1972. After her first purchase of a small primitive horse, Mrs. Dinger then bought twenty carousel horses at one time. However, as she recalls, not everyone was as enthusiastic about merry-go-round figures as she was.

> One of our cars went out of the garage to make room for this menagerie that came in. My friends looked rather aghast at the whole thing, saying "Why did you buy those?" until they saw them. But when I had them up on stands and displayed, they suddenly realized how wonderful they were. It was a rather startling thing to collect at that time because nobody ever thought of it. They didn't realize, I guess, that they were hand carved and they didn't appreciate them. But I felt it was something that should be preserved.

·⤳ Gail Domin ⤳·

Gail Domin, Coordinator of the Urban Cultural Parks Program in Binghamton, New York, was instrumental in making the public aware of the treasure they had in their six Broome County carousels. Ms. Domin relates:

> There was this constant reaching out to the community, that we have something special. I don't think there's anyone locally, in the region, in the vicinity, that doesn't know about our carousels now. That we have six. Why they are important. How expensive they are to restore. Before, I don't think people really understood the importance and the value of the carousels.

Figure 6. Gail Domin, Executive Director of the Susquehanna Urban Cultural Park Commission, reports that the six Allan Herschell carousels in Broome County, New York, are more popular than ever. (Photo: courtesy of Gail Domin)

·⌣ William Finkenstein ⌣·

Artist Bill Finkenstein is well known for his excellent restorations of such carousels as the Lighthouse Point carousel in New Haven, Connecticut, the City Park carousel in New Orleans, and the Roseland Park carousel in New York. R & F Designs, Bill's carousel restoration company, with gross revenues of more than $1 million in 1988, all started with just one horse.

> I was teaching at North Mills High School in Burlington, Connecticut. I taught mechanical architectural drafting and I assisted in the Art Department. Of course, I had a little art

studio on the side. One day, I went home to the art studio, looked out my window and a man was bringing me a horse. He said, "What can you do with this?" I said, "Well, let me see." I worked on it and I gave it back to him. He brought me two more and I worked on those and gave them back and it just kept progressing.

·⁓ Kim Fraker ⁓·

Employee of Six Flags Over Georgia, Kim Fraker tells of that park's Philadelphia Toboggan Company carousel being used in advertising.

A lot of people come out and take pictures of it. It is an antique carousel and it has wooden horses. It's very popular and it's in one of the most attractive spots in the park. I guess it's been about a year ago, Christmas, we did some-

Figure 7. The Ross Park carousel in Binghamton, New York, is the oldest of the Broome County carousels. It was made by the Allan Herschell Company about 1920 and contains sixty horses. The merry-go-round was donated to the city by George F. Johnson, corporate leader of the Endicott Johnson Corporation, with the stipulation that it be operated free of charge to the public. (Photo: Ed Aswad, Carriage House Photography)

thing with Cumberland Mall, which is not too far from here. They came out and brought models and they shot everything for their special Christmas catalog at the carousel and used that as a setting.

·⤳ William Foster ⤳·

William Foster was employed as manager of Palace Amusements in Asbury Park, New Jersey, at the time the 1895 Looff carousel was put up for auction. The historic Palace Amusements building dates back more than a century and was one of the first indoor amusement parks. The historic building is slated to be torn down to make room for condominiums. A "Friends of the Carousel" group was formed to save the carousel, but, as Mr. Foster, reports, there was not enough local interest.

> If there was no interest in the Palace, I told them, "You're not going to get interest in the horses. It's going to be unsuccessful." They wouldn't buy that. They tried and they eventually found out that I was right. People finally came up to me and said, "Oh, it's a shame that the Palace is being torn down." Yeah, I look at them and say, "Well, I don't remember seeing you here for the past three years."

·⤳ Roy Gillian ⤳·

Owner of Gillian's Wonderland Pier in Ocean City, New Jersey, Roy Gillian tells about buying the Philadelphia Toboggan carousel #75 that today is the showpiece of the Pier.

> This came from Sellinsgrove, Pennsylvania. In 1971, there was a hurricane Hazel or Carol or something came through the Pennsylvania area and the Susquehanna River flooded. Flooded this machine and the building started to cave in. So they closed the park. I think for one year the ride was for sale and nobody bought it. Somehow or other a fellow from Baltimore contacted me. They found out I was looking for something. I'll never forget it. I have my own airplane. We flew up there to Sellinsgrove and we went to the park. They had to get rid of it because they then sold the park for development. They had to move this machine. We yanked the boards off. And I remember crawling into the building. The first thing I saw was the swirled brass and my heart started beating and I said to myself, "I have to have this merry-go-round." And, of course, I bought it. I think for

Figure 8. Ninety-nine year old David Gillian worked with merry-go-rounds back in the days when they ran with steam boilers. Mr. Gillian came to Ocean City, New Jersey, in 1914 and opened Gillian's Fun Deck in 1927. Gillian's Wonderland Pier is still in the family. (Photo: Carrie Papa)

$38,000. Today? I was offered a couple hundred thousand dollars for it about five or six years ago. Sight unseen.

·⤳ David Gillian ⤳·

Father of Roy, and ninety-nine years old David Gillian remembers his first merry-go-round.

Them days, we run with a steam boiler. We'd have to get there in the morning and build a fire to get up the steam to run this here engine that had two valves on it. One for the start and one for the brake. That's how I started. With that. We'd go around and play churches. They didn't call them carnivals. They called them church lawn parties.

·⤳ Toni A. Grekin ⤳·

Toni Grekin, Cultural Affairs Director for the City of Binghamton, New York, was asked by the Mayor to make the restoration and the preservation of the Broome County carousels a priority. Toni relates:

About three and a half years ago, the Mayor called me in and said that she had always [as Mayor] wanted to leave these carousels in better shape than they were when she came in. They really had fallen into terrible disrepair. They operated — most of them — but the horses were in very, very bad shape and some of the roofs of the buildings were in bad shape. The first thing we felt we had to do before we even did nuts and bolts was to raise the consciousness of the community in terms of what a treasure they had rather than just taking them for granted.

Figure 9. Toni Grekin, Cultural Affairs Director for the City of Binghamton, New York, on the 1925 Allan Herschell carousel in Recreation Park, Binghamton. (Photo: Ed Aswad, Carriage House Photography)

·⤳ Joyce Hanks ⤳·

When Joyce Hanks joined All Hallows Guild of Washington National Cathedral, Washington, DC, she became involved with the Guild's carousel. The carousel, manufactured by the US Merry-Go-Round Company about 1890, was rescued from oblivion in 1963 when All Hallows Guild members purchased it. Joyce attributes her interest in the carousel to William Manns, as well as to Fred Fried, Marianne Stevens, Barbara Charles, and Nancy Loucks.

> One day when we were getting ready for *Flower Mart*, oh, I guess it's eight or nine years ago now, I was going over to set up and get ready. So, I was over there quite early in the morning and this young man was there photographing and climbing all over it, and photographing it from below and above and so forth. I was fascinated. Finally, he stopped for a minute and introduced himself and said he was William Manns and he was writing a book on carousels, and furthermore, this was one of his favorites. I attribute my interest to

Figure 10. Susan Hofsass and her father, Merrick Price, of Seabreeze Amusement Park, Rochester, New York. Suzy grew up on the PTC #36 carousel that was destroyed by fire in the spring of 1994. Grandaughter of Seabreeze founder George W. Long, Suzy and her dad represent the fourth and fifth generations of Long family involvement with carousels. (Photo: Seabreeze Park)

him. It started there. He was so enthralled with it, he was going to give it a whole page in his book, and sure enough it's page 25 in *Painted Ponies*.

·᠆ Susan Hofsass ᠆·

Granddaughter of Mr. George W. Long, Jr., and daughter of Merrick Price, who now manages Seabreeze Amusement Park in Rochester, New York, Susan Hofsass keeps the carousel animals in good repair. Suzy comments:

> We're all deep into it. At this point, we're running the place. I'm trying to do close to authentic. It's not as perfect as a museum might do. Mr. Long has owned this machine since it was new, so everything that was put on it, he directed at least.

·᠆ Gerry Holzman ᠆·

Master carver Gerry Holzman is the creative force behind the Empire State Carousel, Inc., a non-profit corporation dedicated to the creation of a full size operating carousel. One day, the carousel with accompanying exhibits will become a traveling museum of New York State history and culture. In the following excerpt from his interview, Gerry traces the beginning of the project.

> I had gotten the idea I wanted to do something with a carousel. Being a historian and being a local of New York, I had an extremely rich depository to draw from so I created the concept of the Empire State Carousel, which would embody the whole nature of New York State culture, folklore, and geography. My partner in the wood carving business, Jim Beatty, was very interested in what I was doing. At this point, there's nothing there but an idea and a beaver. I'd carved the scale model of Bucky the Beaver. That's all we had, and the money that we had put up ourselves to incorporate and to begin hiring artists to draw the carousel diagram to make our words have some life. As a little publicity got out, people sent us five or ten dollars, but there was no money of any consequence. I developed a little slide show. I'd go around with the beaver, and I was doing almost missionary work. I'd go around to Kiwanis, and "Y's," any group that would have me.

16

Figure 11 The hand-carved Empire State Carousel is complete and soon could be spinning in downtown Bayshore, New York, to fulfill its motto, *Sic Mundus Festive Circumeat* — "May the World Go Round So Merrily." (Photo: Empire State Carousel)

There was a dinner club nearby in Bayshore. They were thirty couples that met once a month for dinner. So I went there and I showed my slides and showed Bucky the Beaver and they were very supportive, clapped and such. I figured "Well, that's the end of that." And a fellow came up, in his early sixties, very nicely dressed, very pleasant, real gentleman, gentleman of the old school type, and he handed me his card and said, "I'm Dick Selchow of Selchow and Righter, give me a call on Tuesday. I think we might be able to help you get started." So, I called him Tuesday morning and I said, "What did you have in mind, Mr. Selchow? Did you want me to come down and talk to some people?" "No," he said, "I've already talked to our people. We've decided to give you twenty thousand dollars to start the project." So, I went to see him on Thursday. Took the day off from work and he handed me a check for ten thousand and said, "We'll give you the next ten thousand next year."

There were many reasons for his decision. One was, his grandfather had come from Germany in 1867, and started the Selchow and Righter company, which is the same year that Gustav Dentzel hung out his shingle. Dentzel had come from Germany. He saw, from the lecture that I gave, the relationship between the pleasure that the carousel brings and Selchow and Righter, which is a game company. Among their games are *Parcheesi, Scrabble,* and that year, which is sort of just luck, great luck, *Trivial Pursuit. Trivial Pursuit* was going so fast they couldn't keep it on the shelves. They were making so much money from the Trivial Pursuit craze and I came in at that particular point. And they were as good as their word. The following year, there was another $10,000. With that money, we were able to buy wood.

·⁓ Dell Hopson ⁓·

Dell Hopson has been involved with merry-go-rounds and the amusement industry since 1924, when his family moved to Seaside Heights, New Jersey.

I was born in 1910. We moved here to Seaside Heights in 1924. I was associated with the boardwalk in various activities from 1924 on. I was on the boardwalk and around the merry-go-round all the time. I fed the rings to the customers on the merry-go-round. The brass ring. It was a very beautiful merry-go-round, but I don't know what it was. In 1955, we were burned out. We had a very, very bad fire that burned out three blocks of the amusement area.

·⁓ Edward Lange ⁓·

In 1926, Edward Lange started working with various concessions on the boardwalk in Asbury Park, New Jersey. He bought his first merry-go-round in 1935, and purchased the Palace Amusements in 1938. Palace Amusements was one of the first and probably the oldest of the indoor amusement parks in the United States. The original Palace building, which contained a Ferris wheel that went through the roof, was built in 1888. Palace Amusements remained in continuous operation until it was sold in 1986. Today, the Palace building is slated for demolition to make room for luxury condominiums. Mr. Lange remembers the good days at the Palace.

Figure 12. Edward Lange, former owner of Palace Amusements in Asbury Park, New Jersey, always considered his four abreast Loofe carousel "The life, the heart of the business." (Photo: Carrie Papa)

It was great. We had nice people. Nice crowds. It was a very popular resort. We did capacity business. Year after year, we improved. We doubled the size of the Palace. We bought properties adjacent and we made it twice as big. Of course, I always felt that the merry-go-round — it was a beautiful merry-go-round — was the heart of the business. Other rides come and go, but the merry-go-round with the band organ music of course was the heart. When something went wrong with the merry-go-round or the band organ, the place goes dead. The merry-go-round always moves. Even if there were no people, I always told the operator, "If there's nobody on it, move it." And the music. You always had motion, life, the heart. It was the heart of the business.

·⤳ Jane P. R. Lee ⤳·

Washington Cathedral's All Hallows Guild member Mrs. Jane P. R. Lee was the driving force behind the Guild's purchas-

19

ing a merry-go-round for their spring festival "Flower Mart" held on the grounds of the Cathedral each year. In charge of the children's activities at the festival, Mrs. Lee rented a merry-go-round for years. When the opportunity to buy the 1890 carousel, manufactured by the US Merry-Go-Round Company of Cincinnati, Ohio, came up, Mrs. Lee convinced the Executive Committee of All Hallows Guild to purchase the carousel. In this section of her interview, Mrs. Lee remembers the day in 1963 when the Executive Committee of All Hallows voted on the matter.

I called Mrs. Paul Nitze, who was chairman of the All Hallows Guild, which put on this *Flower Mart*, and I said, "Phyllis, we can't rent the merry-go-round this year, and I think we ought to buy it." "Well," she said, "there's an Executive Committee meeting tomorrow at the Deanery, come over." So, I said, "Sure," and I went over and there were all

Figure 13. All Hallows Guild of Washington National Cathedral has an ongoing restoration program to keep their US Merry-Go-Round Company carousel in top condition. Most of the restoration work is done by local members of the National Association of Tole and Decorative Painters. The camel "Pillow" was restored in honor of Jane P. R. Lee, the All Hallows Guild member who obtained the carousel for the Guild and is considered the "mother" of the carousel. (Photo: Karen Smith)

these ladies sitting there. I have always gone in rather heavily for fun, you know the light touch, and I said, "We've just got to have this merry-go-round. I mean your Flower Mart is nice, but I think flowers and spring, you need some music too." This merry-go-round had a lovely caliola, and it's one of the last ones around made by the Wurtlizer people. So they asked me a few questions, and I said, "Well, you know, I just think every cathedral should have its own merry-go-round." Well, they had a good laugh over it, the cathedral needing a merry-go-round. So they thought for a good long time, and then they had a vote. This is funny today when the women's movement has moved so far. One woman who voted against it, on the way out, she said, "Well, I simply cannot wait for you ladies to go home and tell your husbands that you have voted to buy a merry-go-round for the cathedral." Well, that was how it was, "What would your husband think?" But, we bought it, and I told them "It's not just for the children, but," I said, "you're going to see the

Figure 14. Mabel Long, widow of Thomas V. Long, worked right along with her husband in operating Bushkill Amusement Park in Easton, Pennsylvania. Mabel's favorite horse on the last Long machine to be built was "Pistol Packin Mama." When asked why she thought this Long machine was the best of them all, Mabel replied, "Because it's mine." (Photo: Carrie Papa)

biggest difference in the world." And it has worked that way. It sets the tone.

·⤳ Mabel Long ⤶·

Widow of Thomas V. Long of the well-known Long family who built eight carousels between 1876 and 1903, Mabel Long continued to operate Bushkill Park and the last Long machine to be built, until her death in 1989. Although she didn't know the rest of her life would be involved with merry-go-rounds and amusement parks when she met Tom Long, Mabel did realize she had met the right person for her and it was love at first sight.

> On my part and on his too. That was in July, 1932. I met him on the merry-go-round. He collected tickets. I met him through a friend of his. She took me to the park as a guest. We went there on a picnic, and he was operating the machine.

·⤳ George W. Long, Jr. ⤶·

Another member of the Long family, son of George W. Long, Sr., George Jr. started his career in the amusement business when he was seven years old. In the summer of 1898, his father installed a Long machine in Cape May, New Jersey, and George Jr. accompanied him and worked as the ring boy. By 1926, George had purchased his own Philadelphia Toboggan Company carousel and installed it in Seabreeze Park, Rochester, New York. Eventually, Mr. Long was able to buy the entire park from the transit company. About the sale, he relates the following:

> The Transit Company came to me in 1945 and they said, "We're ready to sell now." I said, "How much?" He said, "Oh, I don't know, maybe a hundred thousand." I said, "All right, if I had that hundred thousand, I wouldn't even bother with you. I wouldn't even talk to you." He said, "Don't get excited! We're going to have a competent real estate man look the place over. You can tell him what belongs to you and we'll tell him what belongs to us, and we'll see if we can't work out a deal." I said, "That's fine." So a good real estate man came down and he spent about a month down there, and the railway company came back and said, "We've got a price, eighty-five thousand." So, I said, "Well, if the bank will go along with me, I'll see if I can do business with

22

you." So I go to the bank and I have a friend in the bank. I had borrowed money on several occasions, but I had paid everything back when the depression came. I had accumulated about thirty-five thousand, so I went in to Jardine in the bank and I said, "I have to have fifty thousand just on my signature, how about it?" He said, "Well, I'll have to take it up with the board. I can't okay fifty thousand without talking to the board." So, I said "Okay." So he came back a couple days later and he says, "It's alright." So I went through with the deal. With that fifty thousand and my thirty-five, I bought the thing. And I was able to pay it off in two seasons.

·⸱ Kenneth Lynch ⸱·

Kenneth Lynch, who does the restoration work on many of the carousel pieces in the Charlotte Dinger Collection, started his part-time career as a master carver and restorer because he inherited a garage full of woodworking equipment and unfinished projects. He started making some Queen Anne and Chippendale pieces for himself and then carved a wooden rocking horse for his small son. This led to his eventual restoration of

Figure 15. Kenneth Lynch with the rocking horse he carved for his son in 1982. (Photo: Debora Lynch)

23

thirty-five pieces in the Dinger collection. Ken comments on the skills needed for restoration work and the attachment one develops for the figures worked on.

> Well, you need a lot of patience. Some of the jobs that I've done, working part time, and if they're minor, I can be done within a week or so. The amount of actual hours varies per type of restoration needed. One piece, I probably worked on for over a year. Each piece presents its own problems. Some are very minor and some can be major restorations. There's always a fair amount of tedious type of work involved with each piece. If a piece is in relatively good condition, you try to make it ever better so any type of small little defects, you go over it time and time again to eliminate those. That becomes very, very tedious. By the time I'm a quarter or a third of the way through, it almost becomes my worst enemy because I continually look at things and say, "Well, this could be better, this could be better, this could be better," and by the time I'm through with it, I know the animal, every square inch of it just about, and I really hate to see it go. It becomes like a, almost a part of a child.

·⤳ John MacIntosh ⤳·

For the past fifteen years, John MacIntosh has repaired the animals on the Floyd L. Moreland carousel in Seaside Heights, New Jersey. In the following paragraph, John describes the satisfactions in his work.

> The most satisfying thing for me is to work on horses that real artists have worked on. I mean they're all hand done. There's no argument, they're just a beautiful piece of work. I feel privileged to work on them, to try to match what those people did. I had to do a full leg and that's a challenge to try to make it look exactly the same and come out exactly the same, that's satisfying.

·⤳ William Moore ⤳·

In September, 1989, William Moore was the General Manager of the Six Flags Great Adventure theme park in Jackson, New Jersey. At the time of the interview, Mr. Moore emphasized the importance of the Savage carousel to the park.

> In Great Adventure's history, it's taken a very prominent place. The carousel was the center focus point for the park

as it was originally laid out. The park has changed over the years so it's not in the same center point that it was. The front gates used to all come towards the carousel. Now it's on the center street, and it is still a very prominent feature in the park. And of course we use it pretty regularly in any kind of advertising we do because it creates a certain image about families and kids and those kinds of things. For example, even if we're doing a roller coaster advertisement for a new ride, we're going to put the roller coaster in and maybe three or four rides. Especially, the carousel because it's a joy to photograph. It's always very beautiful. The lights and all. I think when people think of amusement parks, one of the rides that comes to mind very quickly is the carousel.

·꙳ Floyd L. Moreland ꙳·

Dean of Graduate Students and Professor of Classics at City University of New York, Dr. Floyd L. Moreland loved the Casino Pier carousel at Seaside Heights, New Jersey, from his earliest childhood. During his high school and university years, Floyd got a job working on the carousel weekends and during the summers. This is a practice he continues today. Dr. Moreland, his mother, step-father, and a couple friends spent the winter of 1982–1983 bringing the grand old carousel back to its original beauty.

> We did it racing against time. Only on weekends and holidays. This building got colder and colder 'cause there's no heat. Our fingers would sometimes be numb. All day Christmas day, all Thanksgiving day. I would sit on scaffolds from dawn till I couldn't stand it anymore because we knew the summer with the spring would come. We wanted to open and we wanted it to look so differently. It became this great project. What we wanted to do was make the carousel sparkle. I wanted so much, in the spring when we opened, for people to walk in here and "Oooh" and "Aaah." It was a project that I think enriched all of our lives, so I'm very thankful for that. This carousel has done a lot in my life.

·꙳ Merrick Price ꙳·

Son-in-law of Mr. George W. Long, Jr., Merrick Price has been involved with the Philadelphia Toboggan Company carousel at Seabreeze Park, Rochester, New York, for many years. On being a part of the fifth generation of merry-go-round people, Mr. Price comments on the family's interest in restoration and preservation of the carousel figures.

Mr. Long took very good care of them. I think that one of the interesting things is that you never find two horses exactly alike. If you found one with another Irishman on it, it wouldn't be the same. It might be on the front, but it wouldn't be the same because they are all hand done. The guy, that morning, he decided, "Oh, I think I'll do this," and he just laid that out and carved it. As for the future of the Seabreeze carousel, it stays right where it is. We have no plans of ever selling it or moving it. It would be the last thing that we would sell, I'll tell you that.

·~ Albert Reid ~·

Albert Reid is co-owner of Keansburg Amusement Park in Keansburg, New Jersey. In his interview, Mr. Reid explains the differences between his kind of small, family-run amusement park and the great theme parks.

This is different here. Something different than a regular stamped out theme park someplace. We've got personality. We make french fries like they did back fifty years ago. They use frozen fries in the theme parks. And they stamp out a McDonald's hamburger. We make different stuff here. They haven't centrally planned it in some board room. Each park, each amusement park, has it's own personality. But the new ones, the big ones, the rich ones, I really would feel happy just calling them plastic places. It's a commercial product. It's the golden arches of McDonald's. You ever go someplace and have a real good hamburger that's juicy, that you can't eat because it runs down your hand and those fried onions are slipping off and they put lettuce and tomatoes and long pickles on it and the roll is toasted or homemade. That's what you can get in Keansburg. I don't want to pick on them, but we're different here. You have to be here to get the flavor of it, the smells and the noises and the kids exciteness.

·~ Bernd Rennebeck ~·

Born in Germany, Bernd Rennebeck lived near a factory that made roller coasters. After completing his education, he became involved in setting up coasters and larger rides all over Europe,

Japan, South Africa, Russia, and America before opening his own import business in New York. In addition to specializing in large rides such as coasters and Ferris wheels, Mr. Rennebeck imports Italian carousels that are primarily set up in malls. He describes the horses that look like the famous Lippizaner horses of Vienna.

Figure 16. The Venetian carousels imported by Mr. Rennebeck are replicas of the double-decked Phillip Schneider carousel which was built in Germany in 1898. The twenty-eight horses are made from molds of the original Schneider carousel, have genuine horsehair tails, and are hand painted. Italian artists also paint the Venetian scenes surrounding the carousel's upper and lower facade. (Photo: Courtesy Bernd Rennebeck)

We could make copies of American horses, but I think the type of horse we use now fits very well with the general style. They're white, most of them are white, more like the Lippizan stallions. Making them, even the fiberglass, is an art form because you have to make a mold. You have to make an original. the new ones now are a little bit more cleaner looking. The style is a little bit more modern than the older ones. I like any of the ornate, old horses, but I don't like some of the angry looking ones. Some of them are really very angry looking. That's one of the reasons why we modified the horses we use on our carousels now. They are all gentle looking creatures. As I said before, these Lippizan stallions are

27

nice looking, almost smiling horses. All white with colorful trappings on them.

·⤳ Richard Schiess ⤳·

Richard Schiess started working at Palisades Amusement Park in Cliffside Park, New Jersey, when he was sixteen years old. He continued to be employed there until the Park closed in 1978. In the following section, Richie recounts the yearly opening day of Palisades.

Every year for the opening of the park, we used to have parades. All the schools around, Cliffside Park, Fort Lee, and

Figure 17. Palisades tickets and flyer. From flyers to reduced tickets to advertising on match book covers, promotion was constant at Palisades Amusement Park. (From the collection of Richard Scheiss)

all of them, used to come here. They had the school colors. We had the black and the red. Fort Lee had the blue and the white. All the classes from kindergarten all the way up to the ninth grade. And all the kids got some kind of free food, free tickets. Every one of them. That was the big day of the whole thing. The kids couldn't wait to be in the parade and come to the park. I was part of the parade before I started working at the park. The park was great for everybody.

·~ Gary Swarer ~·

Gary Swarer has been in charge of maintaining the Floyd L. Moreland carousel in Seaside Heights, New Jersey, for more than twenty years. In the following, Gary considers the satisfactions and the problems involved in maintaining old equipment.

> In the mechanical aspect, it's satisfying to think of the talent that an individual had to have at that time to manufacture any of the parts for that ride with not having the equipment that's available today. Today, it could be done on computer type machines. Most of this was all done by hand with vials and hand tools and that type of thing and an old forge. Many parts can't be repaired. They have to be reproduced. We have them made by a company that is in Trenton. They've really duplicated everything that was there. That's an art too. That's Marshal Maintenance in Trenton. It took a while to find them. The crank shafts that control the movement of the up and down horses were made probably somewhere's in the 1890s, so that puts them close to a hundred years old. In a hundred years of use, you have metal fatigue. It's being taken apart right now so that a testing company can come in and magnaflux all the shafts. It's a safety measure so that nobody is hurt because of a shaft breaking.

·~ Justin Van Vliet ~·

Both Justin Van Vliet's parents and grandparents were in the carnival business and traveled with their Allan Herschell merry-go-round throughout the northeastern United States. Mr. Van Vliet grew up with the carnival and the carousel. He remembers when his father bought new replacement horses.

> In 1948, my father bought all new horses for the merry-go-round, but they were aluminum horses. They were junk. Threw the old ones out. Threw them out up in Watervliet, New York. We just took them off the merry-go-round, turned them on their backs and left them lay. Thirty-six horses. When I look these flyers over, when I see what they're worth, I could kill myself. But, you can't do nothing about it.

Figure 18. Justin Van Vliet's grandmother Elizabeth and step-grandfather Michael Buck were the proud co-owners of the "SENSATIONAL" B. & V. traveling carnival show. (Photo: Courtesy Justin Van Vliet)

·‿ Charles Walker ‿·

Charles Walker, for several years, has served as Conservation Chairman for the National Carousel Association. As a child, he was fascinated with merry-go-rounds and hoped one day to own one. That opportunity came in 1968.

> This old carnival fella came around and he said, "I know where there's a carousel and it's for sale. The man wants to get rid of it." At that time, I had no money, but I thought, "Well, I'll just go look at this thing anyway and just see." He

said it was a Philadelphia Toboggan, and, of course, that was my favorite carousel. So, I went over to this warehouse, and there were these stacks of horses with big brown eyes looking at me, and I lost control. The man thought that I would be stuck with the carousel and wouldn't know what to do with it and everything. Thought that I would probably sell it back to him. But he was wrong, because I knew, if I got one, my determination would be to get it back together again, no matter what. Had it delivered.

·⤳ Paul Woehle ⤳·

Owner of Fairy Tale Forest in Oak Ridge, New Jersey, Paul Woehle opened his amusement park in the early fifties. At ninety-one years old, he still spends a great deal of time working in the park. Here, he speaks of the beginning.

I told my friend, "I'm looking for some property where I can start a fairy land or something." That was always with me as a little kid. My mother, she was great in fairy tales. She had eleven kids. We were four brothers and seven sisters. Her hobby was to get all the kids together in the wintertime. When it was cold, we were sitting around the stove and she used to tell us all kinds of fairy tale stories. And that always was with me. I always liked that. And I figured someday it would be nice to make the kids happy and get something like that. So I started here. Little by little. We started to build one house after Hansel and Gretel. Then we built in Cinderella, and then Snow White and so on and on. We have the merry-go-round. We have the fire engine. Then we have a helicopter and we have a train ride through the Candyland. The merry-go-round has twenty-four horses on it. It comes from Coney Island. Naturally, I did my work on it too. Whenever I could pick up a nice picture, I copied it and put it on there. Scenery's all around on the inside.

These thirty-seven people you have just met are the "Carousel Keepers" who participated in the oral history project. In their memories we recognize our own recollections of favorite amusement parks and special merry-go-rounds, and experience the pleasure of reliving happy memories of childhood.

2

The Charm of the Past

The great years for the development of the American amusement park — from the turn of the century until the end of World War I — coincided with the Golden Age of the carousel. There may have been merry-go-rounds without an amusement park, but it is safe to say that there were no "pleasure palaces" or parks that didn't feature a carousel. In fact, a merry-go-round placed at the end of a trolly line often was the forerunner of a great park. The steamship lines and railroad companies carried hundreds of passengers to the parks and seaside resorts for a day's excursion or an evening's fun. Between the turn-of-the-century and the First World War, fifteen hundred amusement parks were built in the United States. Then, the Great Depression of the 1930s brought an end to the amusement park boom that would not be duplicated until the 1950s and the rise of the modern theme parks.

At sometime in their life, nearly everyone has visited an amusement park. More than likely it was a small family-owned park, a seaside resort, or a summer gathering place at a nearby lake. Memories of long summer days spent at the local amusement park are revived by the recollections of others as shared experiences are brought to mind. One portrait of the past comes from Albert Reid and the early days at Keansburg Amusement Park.

33

It started back sometime around 1906 or so. A man named William Galehouse owned this area. This point here was filled in by dredges and barges. They made streets out of it, paved it and subdivided it. He owned quite a bit of property. They also owned a bus company, and first the Keansburg Steamboat Company. You can see the poster on the wall over there. That boat is now in a boat yard someplace up in New York. I believe they might be junking it. It's a shame. It's a bit of nostalgia and history. You see in the old days, they didn't have the roads like they have now. Highway 35 was two lanes and it may not even have been paved in certain areas. These boats are called intercoastals, steamers. They were not ocean going, but they went around the coasts. They'd come from New York to here. A lot of the people came by intercoastal steamers, not only here, but in the Great Lakes and farther down the shore. It's part of how amusement parks started.

Around the turn of the century, you'd have a brewery, and you'd have a band stand and they would play the oompha music and marching music. People would come to hear the band concert and drink beer. Then, they started with something for the kids. They'd put in a carousel, and then they'd put in a Ferris wheel. Then they suddenly had a beer garden and an amusement park. Then the breweries went but the parks were still there. We still have something similar. We have the Heidelburg, which is like an imitation of the Octoberfest in Germany. Bar where they serve you bratwurst and beer. This is an eatery here in Keansburg. Right on the boardwalk two doors down. Even today they serve one of the finest hot dogs anywhere.

Bertrand Island Amusement Park in Lake Hopatcong, New Jersey, was run by the D'Agostino family. Almost from the time the park opened in 1922, Raymond D'Agostino's father had concessions at the park. When the opportunity to buy the park came up in 1947, that's what the D'Agostinos did. Having grown up with the business, Ray spent the next thirty years running Bertrand Island, first in partnership with his dad and later on his own.

SCHOOL OUTING INFORMATION

REDUCED RATES ON ALL MAJOR RIDES (20)

EFFECTIVE EVERY DAY, 10 A.M. TO 5 P.M. – EXCEPT SUNDAYS AND HOLIDAYS

SPECIAL REDUCED RATE RIDE TICKETS ARE AVAILABLE TO ALL SCHOOL GROUPS. These reduced rate ride tickets are good for all the 20 Major Amusement rides in the Park. The Roller Coaster, Ferris Wheel, Lost River, etc. These reduced rate ride tickets cost 20 cents each. With one of these tickets anyone in the school group is entitled to a ride on any of the Major Rides. The normal price of the amusement rides ranges from 30 to 50 cents, so it is plain to see the saving each person gets on each of the amusement rides. Each person can purchase as many tickets as desired. The tickets are consigned to the person in charge of the group upon arrival at the park by the Park Manager. This person in turn sells the tickets to their group - a very simple operation taking a matter of a few minutes to complete. The tickets are on rolls and are all serially numbered, so we know exactly what is used, and that is what is paid for. Tickets are also available in books of 20 tickets. If a large group consisting of five or more buses wishes to sell tickets prior to their arrival at the park, arrangements can be made to have tickets mailed in advance by contacting the Park Manager at least two weeks prior to the date of arrival.

EFFECTIVE EVERY DAY PARK IS OPEN
– FREE ADMISSION TO THE PARK
– FREE BUS PARKING
– FREE USE OF PICNIC TABLE FACILITIES LOCATED THROUGHOUT THE ENTIRE PARK

Mail Application below to BERTRAND ISLAND PARK, Box 395, Mt. Arlington, N.J. 07856

APPLICATION FOR BUS ENTRY PERMIT

(No Bus may enter the Park without Permit)

1. *Date of Picnic* .... *Alt Rain Date:* ....
2. *Name of Group* ....
3. *Address of Group* ....
4. *Type of Party: School*....... *Church*....... *Club*.......
5. *Number of Buses* .... *(Permit will be valid for ONE more bus than herein requested. If more than one extra bus is required, phone* Area Code 201- 398-0136 *or write, if time permits.)*
6. *Has this group ever before picnicked at Bertrand Island?* .... *If so, what year* .... *month* ....

....
(Signature of person making above application)

....
(Print Person's Name and Address Where Bus Permit is to be Sent)

PERMITS MAILED ONLY TO "HOME ADDRESSES"

Figure 19. A major part of the business at Bertrand Island Amusement Park was from school groups. Arrangements for tickets and busses were made in advance. (From the collection of Ray D'Agostino)

We did a tremendous school business. We used to get schools from all over New Jersey, and an awful lot of parts of New York, Brooklyn, and as far away as Connecticut. I used to have some days when eighty and ninety bus loads of kids come in here and really have a real good time. A very memorable day. I run into people today, in Florida — I go to Florida every winter for the past forty years — I run into people there and they say, "Oh, did you ever hear of Lake Hopatcong?" And I say "Yes" and they say, "We used to go to an amusement park there as a child." I say, "That's interesting." Wherever I go, I run into people that tell me as a child, as school children, that they used to come to Bertrand Island for a day's outing, for a day's vacation.

The best part of the amusement business was just to hear the people and the kids hollering, screaming, laughing, yelling, having a good time all day long. You forgot the rest of the world was having problems and everything else. You used to stay in the park and listen to all these kids come up with their school teachers and the nuns and the priests. I mean it was just one fun day. That's what it was. Fun all the time for a hundred days.

For many, many years I used to entertain a thousand nuns. Just before my season opened. The Paterson Diocese. The Bishop, he wrote to me, Bishop Navale. They wanted to know if I could have a nice day with just the nuns here. The nuns of all the schools in the Paterson Diocese. I said "Certainly." I would set aside a day when there would be no other people in the park. I usually used to do that a few days before the park opened. But, I would have everything ready. The bishop would come up with several priests, and there would be anywhere from six hundred to a thousand nuns. They would be running around the park, and they were just like kids, riding all the rides, and they would have one good time. It was very, very nice. I thought it was good too, because, you see, those nuns that were coming up that day, many of them were going to bring groups up in May and June and July. Groups of kids. So they would see what was going on here. A lot of them were principals of schools, and a lot of the schools would bring the entire school, from the first grade all the way up to the eighth grade.

I found in my business here, that I did a bigger Catholic school business than I did a public school. When the time

Figure 20. The beach and amusements at Bertrand Island Amusement Park about 1920. (Photo: From the collection of Ray D'Agostino)

came to leave — around four o'clock or so — you would think I was running Vatican City from my office. I used to announce over the loud speaker all the schools that were ready to load their busses to go back home. And I tell you, there were times when I had thirty or forty different Catholic schools and I had to announce all these names. And I'm sure that if anybody that wasn't a Catholic was in the park, they were thinking, "What is this, Vatican City or something," because I was going Saint this and Saint that, and Saint this, your bus is getting ready to load. Your sisters are ready on the bus for you to go home. That's the way we used to do it, every day.

As insurance costs went up many carousel owners abandoned the ring machine. One of the last merry-go-rounds in New Jersey to retain rings was located at the Palace Amusements in Asbury Park. Edward Lange's observation affirms the simple pleasure and excitement the ring machine brought to the merry-go-round rider.

We always had the rings. That was one of our features. We were one of the last ones to have brass rings. Naturally, every ride, you put the brass ring in so that somebody gets a free ride. Sometimes, we would put it in twice. On weekends. The thing goes around anyway, and somebody gets a brass ring, they're happy. Oh, that was a big thing to get the brass ring.

The trouble is, they used to steal them. They wouldn't want the free ride. They kept the brass ring for a souvenir. So, we had to buy a lot of rings. Every year, it was two thousand or three thousand dollars worth of rings we had to buy. Even the steel ones they used to take. And they became more and more expensive. Five thousand and six thousand dollars. But we still kept it because the people came for the rings. The adults. It was a child's ride, but when it came to grabbing rings, then it was a challenge. It was quite an expensive thing, but we always had rings. Always.

The Second World War years were busy ones for the amusement industry. People were working, had money to spend, and looked for enjoyable ways to escape the worries and fears of wartime America. Roy Gillian remembers those days on the pier at Ocean City, New Jersey.

> I was running the merry-go-round during the war years. The fact is, I remember how we used to run. We only had two bulbs in each section of the merry-go-round. We had two coffee cans over them so that the light was down. There were no lights on the Ferris wheel. We just had one little spot where we loaded. All that time during the war, the lights on the boardwalk were all painted black, except a little white spot on the inside that showed a little bit down. Every fourth light was on.

Figure 21. Gillian's Plymouth Place, Ocean City, New Jersey, in 1932. Owner David Gillian is standing by the fence with two of his sons, Dave, Jr. and Robert, working on the ring stand just inside the fence. (Photo: Senior Studio)

> In 1945, VJ Day I guess, Japan, there was such a crowd on the boardwalk out there that our deck caved in. That was towards the end of August when the war was actually over. I'll never forget that as long as I live. There were rolls of toilet paper people were throwing through the Ferris wheel.

Throwing paper off of there. It was just an unbelievable night. People were riding all of the rides. It was just like one big party. I'll never forget it.

The merry-go-round was an innocent and ideal place for young people to meet one another during the proper and restrained years of the early twentieth century. Charlotte Dinger recalls that the amusement park provided a place where friends gathered and romances flourished a few decades ago.

My mother's almost ninety now. She has great memories of carousels and the way things were in Asbury Park in the old days, and how everyone dressed on weekends. So different from today when you think of people in formal clothes walking the boardwalk. She said that she remembers that the men, the young men, would stand around the outside of the carousel and the ladies would ride it and they would kind of look at each other. Kind of flirting. It was a great way to meet. Young people would meet at the carousel.

I have very happy memories of a carousel in particular at Olympic Park in Maplewood, New Jersey. That carousel is one of the grandest carousels in existence. It is now at Disney World in Florida. But it operated in Olympic Park for many years. It's just a fabulous carousel. All horses, but just very elaborately carved horses. Very highly decorated rounding boards and crestings. It's just a magnificent structure. I enjoyed that very much as a child, and always had hoped someday, I'd have a carousel horse of my own. I used to study the horses. I don't think too many people did that, but I remember sitting around the perimeter of a carousel and when it would stop, I would look at the horses and study the carvings. Some of them had eagles and flags. They were very elaborate. That was the beginning of my interest in carousels as more than a ride.

I went there as a child and through my teen years. Then, when I was married, I took my children there. I used to take them with their friends, when they had birthdays. We'd go to Olympic Park because it was an old fashioned amusement park and very well kept. They had a band stand and wonderful old rides, a caterpillar and so on, before the rides were so crazy tipping you upside down and inside out. It was just a very nice place for a family to go.

Figure 22. In 1967, Walt Disney World acquired the antique Liberty carousel, which was shipped to Florida where Disney craftsmen were surprised by the detail and artistic grace they found when years of park paint were removed. (Photo: Walt Disney World Company)

Figure 23. Today the famous Liberty carousel, PTC #46, has been renamed "Cinderella's Golden Carousel" and is one of the most popular attractions in the Magic Kingdom. (Photo: Walt Disney World Company)

The layout and design of amusement parks evolved from the early picnic groves that lured city dwellers to the country for a day's outing. William Moore, former General Manager of Six Flags Great Adventure in Jackson, New Jersey, described the Victorian design of the park.

The park was designed by Mr. LeRoy as a kind of unique attraction. There's a lot of English influence on the park. Our original landscape design person was English. Warner LeRoy is the creator if you will of the original design of the Park. Warner is most noted for Tavern on the Green restaurant in New York. That's his restaurant. He designed that and, he's really credited with the design and original layout of this Six Flags.

The carousel was the center focus point for the park as it was originally laid out. The park's changed over the years so it's not in the same center point that it was. The front gates used to all come towards the carousel.

Figure 24. The Carousel Building at Six Flags Great Adventure, Jackson, New Jersey. "The architecture and style of the park has a Victorian flavor. It was seen as a strolling kind of place where you'd come out on a Sunday afternoon and walk around" — William Moore. (Photo: Courtesy Six Flags Theme Parks)

One of the things he did require is that we left as many as possible of the natural trees and vegetation in place. And that's very unusual. Typically, when a theme park is built, the bulldozers come in, level all the ground, build a park and then plant trees and start over. If you drive through our park, you'll see all around here, plus the park itself, a tremendous amount of trees. That's unique to here.

Mr. LeRoy was a show person. Architectural show. Show from the standpoint of the visual sensations a person might get. It was seen as a strolling kind of place where you'd come out on a Sunday afternoon and walk around. The architecture and style of the park has a Victorian flavor. If you drive around a little bit, you'll see that we spend quite a bit of our energies and finances into the landscaping and upkeep of the park.

Another respondent who commented on the pastoral importance of the park setting is Joseph Bornman, Manager of the Sanatarium Playground of New Jersey. Not an amusement park in the usual sense, the Playgound was established for the benefit of underprivileged children in the Philadelphia area.

It started here in this particular location in 1887. Mr. Waters started it. His son has it now. It's a non-profit organization. It was started by Smith, McCormack people. People find out about it by word of mouth. It is strictly for underprivileged children. We have school kids in here. We run anywhere from four hundred to seven hundred kids per day. It's free. We provide food and milk for them. Milk and crackers at ten and two and soup and crackers at noon. The children come in by bus from Philadelphia. Most of them come out of the city. Primarily underprivileged kids. They come from mom and pop organizations, church organizations, organizations that cater to that type of element, and they are designated to do that type of work. A lot of churches run day camps and things of that nature. Sometimes you have handicapped kids coming in here with wheel chairs and all. It's a variety. It could be black, Hispanic, Chinese, Korean, you name it.

We have a slide and swings and the carousel and two pools. The carousel is the major ride. It has Freidrich Heyn horses

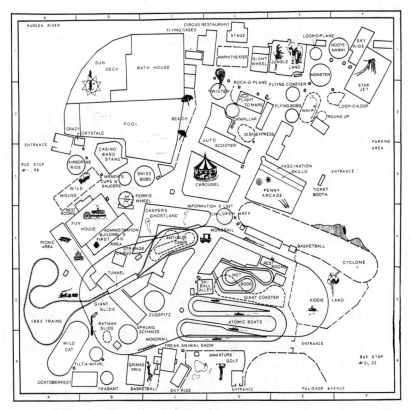

Figure 25. The locator map of Palisades Amusement Park shows the prominent and central location given to their carousel. (Photo: Courtesy of Richard Glasheen)

on it, but this is an American made machine. The carousel is for the kids. The whole thing here is to cater to kids. Kids don't care about antiques. Kids are there to have fun. And they do. When the kids come out of that city, this is probably the only green grass they see. It's an outing where they come out and have a great time. It might make a world of difference in their lives, whether they become totally prejudiced or they realize that somebody does care.

Of course there were times when the "good old days" were not that good. George Long, Jr., a second generation member of the well-known Long family builders of carousels, remembers

43

traveling with his father to install a merry-go-round near Norfolk, Virginia, in 1903.

They found a place in Piney Beach, Virginia, across the bay — that's the Chesapeake Bay — from Norfolk, Virginia. I was there with my father. I was eleven years old at that time. The park never materialized that summer. There was no business there whatsoever, so we had to fish to eat. The fishing was good. We ate fish all summer. Fish and crabs. Hard shelled crabs. We lived in a little shack called a photography gallery, which was erected to be used at the park. There wasn't any loose money in the South in those days. That was terrible. Then the following year, 1904, that carousel was brought to Seabreeze. It was there in Seabreeze until 1926.

See, people didn't have automobiles in the early days. The Transit company ran the lines out. That was great business for them. The park belonged to the Rochester Transit Company. They gave permission to put in the merry-go-round. It was on a rental basis. It was customary to pay 25 percent of the gross to the people who owned the property. After 1914 or 1915 I stayed here. My folks still lived in Philadelphia until about 1920 and then they moved up here too. I studied electrical engineering, but I decided to stay with the merry-go-round. I was introduced to it at the age of seven and I've been with it ever since that time. So, I've had an outdoor life and very good. They were all pretty good years except that one year in 1903, in Norfolk, Virginia. That was terrible.

Seaside Heights, New Jersey, was a more successful beach location than Norfolk, Virginia. To Floyd Moreland, going to Seaside some forty-five years ago was everything a child could wish for.

We came here for as long as I can remember. According to my baby book, I was two the first time. We came with my grandparents, my father's parents. Always for a two week vacation from Passaic. In those days, coming to a place like this was like going to Europe now, or some very exotic place, at least for a child. My parents saved all year, and vacation was a very special focal point in our lives.

Every single day I would ride this carousel. During the daytime, everybody else would be on the beach, and I would want to go to the merry-go-round. Of course at night, that was the big time I'd want to ride it. A lot of kids wanted to run a fire engine [when they grew up] or something, but my big dream was to run the carousel. That, I thought, was just the be all and end all.

The brass ring was right over there. I remember it vividly. On this machine, the outer horses were mobbed. You couldn't get near it. It was a big clown's face with a huge opening where you threw the rings after the ride. There was a boy up there who would keep feeding the rings into a long arm that extended close to the carousel. Then, as it turned, you would reach out and grab. If you got the brass ring, you got a free ride. A lot of people would try to get two or three or four rings at one time. They came out very fast. They were all stacked up inside the rod, so as you pulled one out another would fall right in it's place.

I was able to get a job on the carousel the summer I was on my way to college. Of course one could get a job on the

Figure 26. Although most of the animals on the Floyd L. Moreland Historic Carousel at Casino Pier, Seaside Heights, New Jersey, are horses, it is classified as a "menagerie" since it also has a lion, a tiger, a donkey, and two camels among its figures. (Photo: Dr. Norma B. Menghetti)

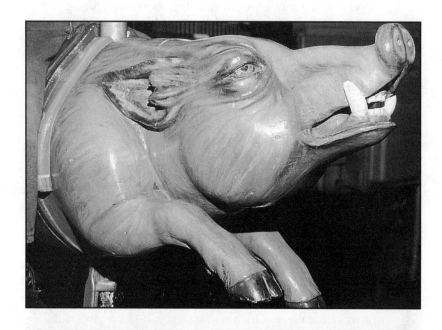

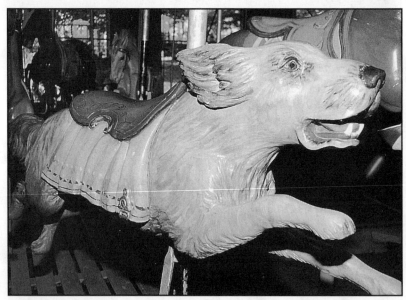

Figure 27. Close-up views of the detail of the ferocious wild boar and leaping dog on the Highland Park carousel in Endwell, New York. (Photos: Ed Aswad, Carriage House Photography)

boardwalk, or on the rides, or in the arcades, but I only wanted one specific job. I remember that first day very vividly. The duties involved starting and stopping and taking the tickets. It was sheer fun for me. I would have done it for nothing. I was getting minimum wage and I needed the money to pay for my education, but it was also just fun. Other people might want to go play baseball or do something else for recreation, but this was my recreation. In those days, the carousel meant something a little different from what it means to me now. Since then, I've learned a great deal about its history and significance. In those days, it was primarily just a magical machine on which dreams could come true.

Between 1919 and 1930, George F. Johnson, the Johnson of the Endicott Johnson shoe manufacturing empire, donated six Herschell Spillman carousels to the various communities in Broome County, New York, where his manufacturing plants were located. A progressive leader, the Endicott Johnson company acted as patron and protector of their workers. The company provided low cost housing, medical services, and parks for the benefit of their employees. George F. Johnson, "the most amazing man you probably never heard of," which is the shoe manufacturer's current national advertising slogan, began his career in the shoe industry at the age of ten, working sixty hours a week for three dollars. With his own background in poverty, George F. Johnson gave the six carousels with the understanding that the municipalities never charge money for the magic ride. Today, the price of admission is one piece of litter. Toni Grekin, Cultural Affairs Director for the city of Binghamton, explains:

> This is a very old policy. This is not a ten-year-old policy or a fifteen-year-old policy. This is an old, old policy. We weren't sure whether this could be assigned to him [George F. Johnson] directly or it just became policy at the same time. [We had] training sessions for all of the park employees that were going to run the carousels. One of the wonderful questions that was asked to me during the training session was "Do we really have to force a four-year-old to bring a piece of litter?" I said, "You absolutely do. But don't think of it in terms of that being a negative thing. You're not forcing the

four-year-old to bring you a piece of litter. What you're doing is helping that child own that carousel because you're bringing him into proprietorship, and part of the proprietorship of that carousel in our community has been helping to keep the park clean. And when you tell him, we'll wait for you and you can get the next ride or whatever it is, just take your time, but you do need to bring it, you are helping him own that carousel for the rest of his life. You are not doing something negative, you are doing something positive for that child."

Children go to our parks, get on a swing, jump into the pool, get their shorts back on and jump on the carousel. It's not like a special trip to see the carousel. It was part of everyday life after school. The carousels are open from twelve o'clock in the afternoon in Binghamton until eight o'clock at night and a kid could ride it all day long if he wanted to. Not for a nickel, not for a dime. There was no money that transpired at all because of Mr. Johnson's commitment. Marion Stickel, in Endicott said, "There were no malls. The park is where the action was."

Part of what we very much want to preserve here is that you can share inter-generationally with part of our community's history. There are not so many things you can do that with. We have a woman who donated two thousand dollars for a horse who has not lived in this community for forty years. She's in New Hampshire. She wanted some young girl to have the same pleasure of riding the same horse that she rode then, hearing the same music that she heard then. How many things can you do when you can say "when I was young," and you can take your grandchild too and know that some other child is having that same pleasure. We're talking something that reminds them of a gentle, warm place in their childhood.

I just focus very specifically on this tour group of senior citizens that came through our community, and I was asked to speak to them. I brought them over to the Rec Park carousel, and it wasn't a question of helping some of these people on the horses, it was a question of helping them on to the carousel itself in terms of their being aged and that infirm. They got on that carousel and — it's not just children, you know — they got on that carousel and the music started up and the lightness that took over their faces. . . . Whatever else happens in your life, there are not so many things that instantly take away the burdens of the hard parts of life as a carousel ride can. It's a simple pleasure. These people, some of them said they had not been on a carousel in forty-five years. And to just see what happened to their bodies when they did this, for that moment of pleasure. I remember — I'm getting mushy now — but I really remember feeling that that's what it is all about.

Gail Domin, Coordinator of the Urban Cultural Parks Program for the Broome County parks, worked with Toni Grekin to raise funds to restore the carousels donated by George F. Johnson. Gail concurs with Toni that:

> It's impossible to be sad when riding on a carousel. It doesn't work. It works against it. I have that same emotional sense because I rode them. I've often thought I have to get money to help repaint them and stuff because I'm responsible for wearing a lot of those saddles thin. I lived in this area and I rode several of them, many, many, many times. That's all we did. The generation behind me will tell you that and the generation now.
>
> I'm a Southsider of Binghamton so I rode the one at Ross Park Zoo the most, but my grandparents lived in a EJ home in Endicott — on my mothers side — so I rode both of them. Two in Endicott. And once I got older and spread out of the neighborhood, I got to Rec Park quite often. He put the carousels in parks very close to the neighborhoods and the factories so people didn't have to commute. He built fire houses for his factories and the neighborhood. Many of the churches, he donated the land or forms for the constructions. Medical facilities, rec facilities. In their home library, they had a lot of Americanization classes for the immigrants for language and kitchen. All kinds of things.

One of the great amusement parks on the East Coast was Palisades Amusement Park in Cliffside Park, New Jersey. Ranking with New York's Coney Island or Chicago's Riverview, Palisades opened in 1922, and remained a favorite with thousands and thousands of patrons for more than half a century. Narra-

Figure 28. During the winter at Palisades Amusement Park, Cliffside Park, New Jersey, Richie Scheiss (right) was kept busy with maintenance. (Photo: From the collection of Richard Scheiss)

tor Richard Scheiss started working at Palisades Amusement Park when he was sixteen years old and remained with Palisades until the park closed in 1970. In his words, working in an amusement park was:

> A fun job. You met a lot of people. At that time, I was making one-hundred-fifty dollars a week on average 'cause I worked long hours. From when the park opened at twelve o'clock till twelve at night. Six days a week. I was off one day. That was just in the summertime. In the wintertime, when we closed the park up, I worked from eight o'clock until four-thirty. The maintenance was done then. On the

carousel, we stripped some of the paint off and made it back to the original. All the different colors that belonged in there and a coat of shellac. I liked the summertime. I like people. In the wintertime, there were forty or fifty employees at the most. In the summertime, maybe five hundred or more. If it rained, you worked a half a day. You got paid the days you worked. The park closed in the rain.

If you worked on the midway, when you would go down by the merry-go-round, you would smell the popcorn, the caramel and everything right there. The stands were right by the merry-go-round. You could smell them as you walked down. There were a lot of stands. Game stands and food stands. A lot of variety of everything.

You could bring your own lunch if you wanted. They had a little picnic area. People used to do that. Bring their lunch and have a picnic. Then go on the rides. Things gradually changed. Went up. Tuesdays and Thursdays at that time were "Bargain Days." The rides were five and ten cents. After six o'clock, they were ten cents. The busiest days were Tues-

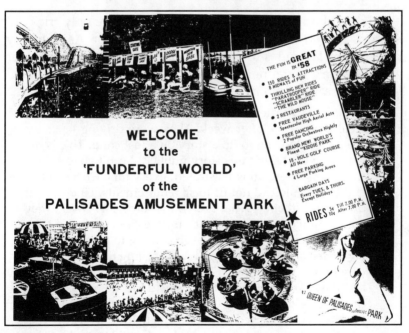

Figure 29. Palisades Amusement Park was so much fun that Richie Scheiss would spend his day off at the park. (Photo: From the collection of Richard Scheiss)

51

days and Thursdays, because of "Bargain Days." Maybe seven thousand or more people on those days. That park was pretty big. Plus, you've got the pool, the people in the pool. Shows going on. Free shows. Something going on all the time. [On my day off] I'd go watch the shows. I'd say to a friend, "Let's go watch the show. I'm off today." I'd go see what's going on.

They sang Happy Birthday to me over the loud speaker. That was the biggest day I ever had. Sol Abrams and Hal Jackson made the plans. Somebody knew it was my birthday, and they sang it over the loud speaker. It went all over the park. And, oh, I was blushing. "Hey, Richie, they're singing your song." I said, "You're kidding." "They're going to sing it." And they sure did. I just turned eighteen. It was really something. Everybody was looking at me, "Ha, now we know how old you are." The park was great for everybody, you know. It was like a family. A family of people. Everybody knew each other.

Singing happy birthday to Richie wasn't the only trick Sol Abrams played over the Palisades loud speaker. As Publicity Director for Palisades for some thirty years, Sol did whatever was necessary to get news coverage for the park, and particularly to get a story in *Life Magazine*.

One year, [writers from] the old *Life Magazine* came out week after week after week. They were driving us crazy. They were looking to do a story on a lost child. This is the first time I'm telling this story publicly. I can't go to jail for this now. I was getting frustrated. Every time we had a lost child, the child did not fit their requirements. Finally, I sat down with them. "What are you looking for?" Well, they wanted a red-headed kid with freckles and such and such and such an age. They had been coming to the park about eight weeks at this time, and I was wasting time. They were driving me up the wall. Finally, I walked around the park one day, like a casting agent. I saw a kid there, and while the parents were looking up in the sky someplace, I grabbed the kid. The kid started crying. I brought the kid in. Boy what a kid. I said, "I found the kid. He was lost." They said, "This is the kid we're looking for." We broadcast over the public address. The parents came in to find the kid. The kid was crying. The whole bit. And that's how I got into *Life* [that week.]

Carousels and traveling carnivals were important to the local residents in the towns they visited. Mr. Van Vliet recalls:

We had one fair and every time we would play there it rained. We couldn't get the merry-go-round on the fair ground because it was too muddy. And those poor people, they wanted a merry-go-round in the worst way. Well, they told my father [by telephone] "We've got to have a merry-go-round." So my father said "If it rains, we can't get the trucks on the ground." They said, "We'll have a hundred men there to carry that merry-go-round on. My father said, "If I see fifty, you'll get your merry-go-round." We drove up there — in fact I was pulling the truck with the merry-go-round — I pulled in and there wasn't a hundred men. There was two hundred men, including women and boys. They did it voluntary, cause they wanted a merry-go-round at this fair.

Down in this area [urban], you had too many distractions. You had movies. But, we'd get up in the rural area, that was your big doings. Like this Afton, New York. This was when I was about nine. They played the fair up there and my father and mother got up and he looked out the tent and it was raining. So, he told my mother, "Go back to bed, it's pouring out there, whose going to come out?" He's laying there and all of a sudden he hears somebody, "Aren't these people going to open up today or what?" Naturally, the farmers couldn't work in their fields. And my father said that was one of the best days they had. Because the farmers couldn't work in the field, they all came to the fair. They were running around there in the pouring down rain. They had slickers on. That was Afton, New York. In those days up in that area, that was something to look forward to. For the farmers that was the big doings.

Many families who owned or leased the small traditional amusement parks had their homes right in the park. Scott Bittler, a fifth-generation member of the Long family, declares that growing up in Eldridge Park, Elmira, New York, was a good experience.

As a small boy, I guess I was raised in the park. The Eldridge Park history dates back to around 1910, and was in continuous operation from something like 1916, when my grandfather restarted activity at the park. Originally, his father had it before him there. This article from the *Elmira Advertiser* from a Tuesday morning of May 17th, 1910, it's headline is *ELECTRIC MERRY-GO-ROUND TO BE INSTALLED AT ELDRIDGE PARK.* Note that they're highlighting the fact that it's electric. It talks about the erection of a building eighty by eighty feet which "will cover a new $10,000 electric merry-go-round. The building will cost $2,000, and it will be erected on the site of the old merry-go-round. The merry-go-round will be the finest in this section of the country. Much larger than the old one and it will be practically noiseless because it's of course electric."

This carousel building was built from scratch by my grandfather. It was an octagon shape from the midpoint up and square at its base. It had an octagon cupola, in other words, at the top, with a flag pole and so forth. Square at the base. Some eighty feet on a side. A very large building. The carousel itself was fifty feet in diameter. One of the largest platforms of carousels. It was a three abreast, but a very large diameter. The carousel mechanism was not the great ornate nature that you find with many carousels, with not nearly the valuable intricate carvings and so forth that many mechanisms had. To some degree, that was by design. My grandfather was of the strong opinion that a carousel's beauty was in its animals, not the mechanism. He, by design, built himself, assembled himself, a ride that definitely focused very clearly on the animals and not on the ornateness of the cornice and the inner mirrors and the inner surroundings so it was a very plain inner circle on the ride.

The building was an entire wood structure with the traditional shape. My grandfather was real proud of it. But, it did not have any means of conveniently closing it up at night to protect it from weather or vandalism or anything of that sort. All the sides were open except the back side which contained some storage area, and, at one time, it was a shop. Its original purpose was to house a very massive band organ, much bigger than could be fit in the center of the ride. It was actually at the back of the building, with its facade open to the ride. Ultimately, gosh, it was either sold or given away or something. We did have a band organ probably to the early 1960s.

Since that time, we have not had a band organ at the Eldridge Park machine, but instead the music came from recorded tape. Most predominantly, the music my grandfather elected to play was big band music, rather than band organ music. That's somewhat non-traditional, but it's also something that marked a pretty unique signature about the ride. Many people would tell you that they came to the park for the purpose of hearing the music only. In fact, it was not uncommon in the evening to find older couples in the merry-go-round building dancing to the music in the area around the ride itself. Big band music was a big thing there.

I think the other thing that set apart our ride was its speed. Many carousels that you find operating at theme parks today don't have ring machines and they operate very slowly. They turn very slowly in many cases. I think we had a couple things that really jazzed our operation up. It had some peppy music. It had the rings, and it turned fast. It was, I would venture to say, the fastest speed of any merry-go-round that I know. I mean, it moved. It got up and went. And, I think, that kind of generated a bit of excitement in and of itself. It kind of gave it a spirit of being alive that some merry-go-rounds just didn't seem to have.

One of the reasons my grandparents lived there during the summer was to be close and be able to hear about things going on, and go down and check in from time to time. [They] lived in an apartment over top of a workshop on the back side of the spook house, which was adjacent to the merry-go-round. I often lived right there with them during the summer and would help out anywhere I could basically. That typically included duties such as maintenance duties, cleanup kinds of duties. Collecting tickets and so forth, that was just some good time. I really miss those days.

A few years ago, much of social life in the summer time did indeed center around the small hometown amusement park. Sadly, Eldridge Park, Palisades, Olympic, and many of the other parks mentioned in these memories have all disappeared. The loss of these fine old amusement parks is much regretted by everyone who remembers their charm and the fun-filled days they offered.

3

That's a Lot of Nickels

Delightful as the atmosphere was in the amusement park and around the carousel, making a living in the amusement industry meant a lot of hard work. The season was short and the hours were long. Inevitably, a great deal of strenuous physical labor went into maintenance, which was daily and continuing. Polishing the brass poles, repairing the horses, and keeping the band organ running were carousel chores mentioned by many of the narrators. However, even those who started working at a very early age, rather than resenting the unending labor, seemed to take pride in doing a good job. Scott Bittler, grandson of Robert A. Long, Jr., says:

> I definitely did not participate in a lot of the normal things that a kid would get involved in in growing up. I had a lot of responsibilities at an early age. I don't think — I don't resent it at all. I'd like to think that I'm a better person as a result of the influences that I had that way, the responsibility I was given, and the influence that my grandfather had a whole lot to do with. I became a ring boy very early. Our carousel — our merry-go-round as we always called it, we never called it a carousel — had a ring machine that was made by my grandfather.
>
> It was originally of the form that had continuously fed rings of an iron variety that were manually fed by the ring boys, as we called them, and would continuously be caught by the outside riders, and then thrown into a big barrel that

Figure 30. "It was attractive to both young and old, just the thrill of being able to catch this thing that gave you a free ride" — R. Scott Bittler. (Photo: The Chemung County Historical Society, Elmira, New York)

Figure 31. R. Scott Bittler proudly displays the Denzel horse he personally restored in the 1970s. (Photo: Courtesy R. Scott Bittler)

was right in front of the ring feeder. On the next time around, they would throw them into the barrel and then catch another one. And every so often we would insert in the series of rings coming through the feeder a brass ring, and, of course, the brass ring would give you a free ride. It was attractive to both young and old, just the thrill of being able to catch this thing that gave you a free ride. Even though the ride was just a quarter or whatever, certainly not a prohibitive price to pay for another ride. Just the thrill that you were the one on the ride, the only one out of dozens of people or hundreds even on the ride, that got the brass ring was kind of a thing that set you apart and made you special. And it was something you could take home if you wanted to or use for another ride and another opportunity to catch yet another ring.

We spent all winter, every winter, restoring the merry-go-round. In fact, the figure you see here with us in the dining room, the Dentzel horse, is a horse that I personally restored, almost by hand entirely. I'm pretty proud of that. It was the primary out of school occupation that my brother and I had during our teens, working in the shop. We would go down after school and on weekends and work in a heated shop area with our grandfather. Often just the three of us there working, sometimes with a couple of other workers. It was a lot of hard work, no doubt about it, but it's something we took a lot of pride in. The summers and the enjoyment of the people on the ride was the payoff.

It definitely cut into social life. We're talking about an operation that we would be up working until very often till one o'clock in the morning in the earlier days when the park was thriving. It was not uncommon for the park to be up and running well into the wee hours of the morning. So, when you don't get off work until one or two in the morning, it's difficult to have much social life, when you've got to be up at six o'clock the next morning to begin to clean up the park and do maintenance work on the park before it opens at noon. So, it definitely cut into our social life. But, by the same token, I met my wife there so, obviously, there was a good thing that came out of it as well.

We didn't have a set closing time at the park. We closed when people left whatever time that happened to be. The park would faze out, closing down gradual rides as people

Figure 32. Robert A. Long in his workshop. As grandson R. Scott Bittler says, "It was a lot of hard work, no doubt about it, but it's something we took a lot of pride in." (Photo: R. Scott Bittler)

kind of left. Typically, the merry-go-round was the next to the last thing to close and the putt-putt golf course was the last thing to close.

I can remember during large industrial picnics that we would have on weekends — this kind of illustrates how crowded the ride got. Unlike many operations where there was a gate around the ride, and you would sell the tickets and collect them as people entered the ride, we didn't practice it that way. We didn't want the ride to be so enclosed. The ride was open. That is, you could get on the ride from anywhere around it. There was no gate that you had to go through to get on the ride. We kept it that way on purpose. The way we would operate is that tickets would be sold in a ticket booth in the building or, in some cases, as with pay one price concepts in parks, a person had an arm band on, and they would just get on. Between rides just get on with either a ticket or arm band, and then the operator of the ride — typically there was more than one, two or three of us boys and sometimes our sisters as well — we would go around and collect the tickets as the ride was running, or just check to see if they had an arm band in that case. Then, when we were done collecting tickets and when the time was up, we would stop it. But to give you a feel for how busy it was, very often on these big weekends, we would have so many people on the ride that it would just take a long time to start up because there was so much weight on the ride. Literally, every horse would be filled and every pole. There would be, like on the outside row, there would be a pole between every horse that one could stand by and pick rings or just stand there in general. There would be at least one person, often two or three people, on every one of those poles between the horses. There would be two or three people in the chariots. Again, on the inside row, there would be poles between each horse and there would be a person on each one of those poles. There were just so many people on the ride, that we would be hard pressed to collect all the tickets within the time limit of the ride with four people collecting tickets on the ride. We would be hard pressed to finish in time to turn the ride off and get another one going. Those were the kind of heydays that I remember and boy that was fun. We just had a ton of fun doing that.

George Long, Jr., at what was then called Dreamland Park, in Rochester, New York, confirms the popularity of the merry-go-round and the amount of work involved in the amusement industry.

We used to have good Sundays at five cents a ride and take in two hundred and fifty dollars. That's a lot of nickels. You bet it is. That's five thousand riders.

Way back then in the thirties, a man by the name of Walker operated a refreshment stand at Dreamland, and he said, "I made a deal. We're going to take the bumper cars up to the Batavia Fair." And I said, "Why did you do that?" "Oh," he says, "it will be a good little business after the season's over at the park." I said, "Yeah, but think of the amount of work." Anyway, he arranged for the bumper cars to go up there. Well, at that time, the cars weighed about six hundred pounds each. They are now down to about three hundred. And I said, "Oh, that's a job. What are you going to do about the steel floor?" "Oh, we'll just take up the steel floor here and put it up there for a week." I said, "I'm going to evade you!" Equipment was so heavy in those days. Steel plate was about eight foot long or ten foot long and three foot wide, and you had to cover the whole floor with steel to get the ground for the cars. They had to connect with the plate for one side of the electric circuit. But anyway, we did it for about five years at the Batavia fair. Then they organized a fair for Lockport, which would come about a week later. So we rode to Batavia and then to Lockport. Covered the two fairs with the bumper cars. Made money, but, oh my, that was hard work. Oh, too much!

The money we spent in those days doesn't mean much in today's figures so it's pretty hard to understand. Of course, to bring a [carousel] machine up here maybe cost a hundred dollars freight. With father and myself helping and probably one extra helper, we would set the carousel up. So, I learned at an early date to be good on helping to do that work.

We had three coasters in there at one time and the Jack Rabbit Coaster that we have now is the best. It's the best ride. That was put in there in 1921. I think practically every stick on it has been replaced. Maybe a couple times in the years that we've had it. We keep it up in fine shape.

We had good years way back when the kids had to almost walk down to Seabreeze Park in the month of May. But, we've always had good service with the transit company. The automobile, of course, brought more people. The automobile has always brought more than the busses ever did.

Justin Van Vliet declares that traveling with a carnival also involved working at an early age, hard labor, and long hours.

Both of my parents were in the carnival business, as well as my grandfather and grandmother. They used to move a carnival known as the B & V Shows throughout the northeastern United States. I started working before I was a teenager. I used to pick up balls, set up cats in my mother's ball game. I would get paid either a quarter to fifty cents a night. All depends on how business was. Business was bad, something like that, you didn't get paid at all. Of course, I was working for the concern, see. [Laughter]. Then later on, as I got older, I started moving the equipment. My favorite ride to move was the Ferris wheel. I used to take that up and down almost every week.

Now a Ferris wheel, if I had what they call a good "top" man, who used to pull the pins to take the spokes out, if I had a good top man, I could drop the Ferris wheel down and on the ground and in the truck in less than an hour. Putting up a Ferris wheel took a little longer. You could do it in about an hour and a half. But then, you'd waste another half hour because you had to secure the Ferris wheel with cables.

Figure 33. Justin Van Vliet, Sr., in the early 1920s. Justin, Jr., reports that the fence around the merry-go-round was made from the crates the horses were packed in for moving. By the late 1930s, the horses were shipped on racks with a truck used only for this purpose. (Photo: Courtesy Justin Van Vliet, Jr.)

To drop a Ferris wheel, all you need is four men. Two for pulling the spokes, the man that works the rope, which would be me, and the top man. During the war years, my older sister used to be my top man. She used to pull the pins and stuff like that. Men were short so all the women did things.

Every night when you shut the carnival down, you took three seats off the top of the Ferris wheel so there was less wind resistance. Every night. Three seats off. Set them on the ground. And then put those empty spaces up on top so that it would cut down wind resistance if a storm came up during the night. Now, if you saw a bad storm coming up, we would take five seats off. Now to get those five seats off, you had to have a couple men climb to the top of the wheel to balance the weight to bring the Ferris wheel around. I operated a Ferris wheel for years. That was my favorite ride. If you had twelve seats, you had to start loading number one and number seven. We hired a man one time. Was supposed to be a Ferris wheel operator. So, I stood and watched him a bit. He started loading one, two, three, four, five. He was so far up, the wheel started coming back down 'cause it was driven by a cable. I told him, "I thought you ran a Ferris wheel." He says, "Yes." "Well, how come you're loading six seats in a row?" "Well, that's the way you're supposed to do it." So, we had him work one night and we got rid of him. He wasn't no good.

Then, the other ride that I worked on was the merry-go-round. I worked on them all. I knew them all inside and out. The merry-go-round, I didn't care much for that. Once you put it up, you used to take another three hours to dress it up. I mean we had to polish the brass. All the jumping horses had brass. We had the largest merry-go-round on the road or truck show. Allan Herschell machine. It had wooden horses. It was a forty foot machine that was made about 1920–21. Most of the Allan Herschell machines were made for trucks. They came apart piece by piece. The main driving gear had seven pieces. In fact, we used to call them the "Seven Sisters" because it was a seven piece gear drove together on the sweeps and that drove the merry-go-round. You put up what they called an A frame and block and tackle. We got all the men around to help pull the rope because the little truck it went too fast. And then you put the merry-go-round up, the center pole. Once you got the center pole up, then you start putting your sweeps in. Then you put your platforms on and set up. Once you got your platforms on, next you put the horses on. The horses just hung on. They had what you call a telescope. All of our horses were jumpers. There's thirty-six horses on that machine. What we did, it's referred to in the carnival as the pig iron. We moved the pig iron. That's the Ferris wheel, the chair plane or the merry-go-round — that's more wood than iron.

The merry-go-round was another thing to take down, because you had to take all those light bulbs out and stuff like that. That was kind of a problem because if you got somebody didn't know how to get the base, like the cornice, they'd jerk them, snap the thing. So when you go put the merry-go-round up the next morning, I was rewiring the merry-go-round more than anything else because they just pulled the plug. They just pulled them apart, so I had to go fix them all the time. After you got the whole thing up, you started adjusting everything. This and that. But we had a beautiful machine.

I was a jack of all trades. As far as I can remember I used to get up maybe eight, eight-thirty. On a weekend, you would go, I would say almost twenty-four to thirty-six hours straight. It all depends on how big a haul we had. Sometimes, I'd be eating supper at nine o'clock. Who had problems here. Who had problems there. Figure on a Saturday, you had your matinee in the afternoon, anywhere from one to four o'clock. Then you shut down for supper hour. Then you start again operating at seven o'clock. But naturally, we had to start before because we had maintenance. Maintenance. You did more maintenance than I think some people do on their homes. The merry-go-round, you're always painting. Each day, the brass had to be polished. Twice a day, when you had the matinees. Naturally, everybody had to grease and oil the merry-go-round, because of all the jumping horses. Like I said, the merry-go-round was the worst for maintenance. It was a job because it was too complicated. There, you had a clutch had wooden blocks in it. My father was the only one knew how to adjust that thing. He tried to teach me. I never could get it. Maybe twice a week that had to be readjusted 'cause the wooden blocks would wear down.

I remember one time, I had to put all new wooden blocks in, and I said, boy, I was glad he was there when we put them in, because I wouldn't never be able to get 'em back. But we got it. On Labor Day we used to open up at nine o'clock in the morning 'cause the farmers came out early. About ten o'clock the merry-go-round operator hears this bang. One of these gears — I mentioned the seven piece gears — we didn't have a replacement for it. Labor Day, where do you get a part? Well, we took it out and I went all over town trying to find a welder to weld it. Actually you had to braze it because it was cast iron. You can't weld cast iron. I couldn't find one. Finally, I go back to the fair and there was a man there had acetylene torches all set up. Brazing outfit all set up. So, I went up to him with the gear — I had one of my men with me, I'm carrying one part of the gear, he's carrying the other part. I told him, "I've got a problem." "Well, I can't help you. I'm selling this stuff. I don't know how to work it." So I lied like a . . . . I never did no brazing in my life. I said, "Well, I know how to work it. I need the rods and stuff." "Well, that's no problem." So, he sent one of the men back to the garage. I said, "I'll tell you what, how long is it going to take your man to get back?" "About fifteen minutes." I said, "Alright, you set up a sign, there's going to be a brazing demonstration." I says, "You're going to have a brazing demonstration and I'll do the brazing." So, within fifteen minutes, his man was back. He put up a couple big signs and I'm doing the brazing. To be truthful, I didn't know what I was doing, but I seen other people and I brazed the gear together. Cooled it off. Got it back and put it in the merry-go-round. Quarter of ten when that gear broke. Quarter of eleven, the merry-go-round was running again. So we ordered a new gear piece for that, but it was two weeks coming from Allan Herschell so that was almost two weeks that gear was running in there with that brazing.

I seen a few times, like upstate New York, we opened for the matinee. We didn't even close the matinee. We just ran right on through. Just changed the price for the ride because at the matinee, it might be five cents for the merry-go-round. Of course I'm talking about many years ago. Five cents to ride the merry-go-round. Then at night it went to ten cents.

Raymond D'Agostino of Bertrand Island Amusement Park in Lake Hopatcong, New Jersey, is yet another respondent whose early childhood was connected with working at the park. Ray also stresses the need for personal involvement to keep everything running smoothly.

I used to come up here every summer. I used to go to school in the winter and every summer I used to have to come up to Bertrand Island and that was my job. I didn't know there were vacations when you could go to the shore. I always knew you just had to come up here and go to work. And that's what I did all summer for years and years as a young boy. I just grew right up into it.

When I ran this park, I was here in the morning at seven o'clock and I used to stay until twelve o'clock at night. I had my fingers on everything. The operation. And the operation was going very nicely. I watched everything going on. I lived very close to the park. The park is only a few minutes away. My wife used to say, "I remember when you came home for supper. You used to call me, and I used to have to have the supper on the table." Within fifteen or twenty minutes, I'd be right back down at that park to make sure that I was there all the time seeing that things were going the way they should go.

It was a seasonal business. We always said we had a hundred day season from Decoration Day to Labor Day. The involvement with the park was at least nine months of the year. During the summertime, I had no vacation. But when we closed Labor Day, we used to have at least two or three months of work that had to be done for the following season. All the work that we could do in the fall, we used to do. Either repairing or building new picnic tables, fixing our buildings, any buildings that had to have roofs taken care of. We owned all the buildings in the park. We used to have to repair roofs. We used to have to repair windows. We used to have to repair paint jobs. Of course, our painting we used to save mostly for the spring. But whatever we could do in the fall, we would because the spring used to be a lot of rain, and you didn't know how much you could do. But during September, October, and a good part of November, while the weather was good, we kept a crew on and did at least three months work after the park closed.

"Blue Monday
and Friday, too,
Banished"

—at—

Bertrand Island Park
Lake Hopatcong's Center of Amusement

Mondays	**Fridays**
All Rides (*except boats*) · · 5c	All Rides (*except boats*) · · 5c
Ball Room Admission · · · 20c	Ball Room Admission · · · 20c
FREE DANCING	FREE DANCING

BECK BROTHERS SPEED BOAT SERVICE

Provides Bargain Boat Transportation
Between

River Styx and Bertrand Island Park

25c Every Monday and Friday Nite Round Trip Fare 25c

This Special Low Rate Applies on Monday and Friday Nights Only

Motor Boat Leaves Following Docks Between 8 and 8:30 P. M.

Pagoda - Mad House - Deane Inn - Sheppie's
Bon Air Lodge - Green Croft

Returning Leaves Bertrand Island at 11:15 P. M.

Figure 34. Martin Kane, President of the Lake Hopatcong Historical Society, recalled the delight of going to Bertrand Island Amusement Park by boat. He said, "From the 1940s on, people came by boat. They put in private boat docks, so it became a big thing for the family to do. Dad would pile all the neighborhood kids into the boat and take them over to the amusement park. It was a big treat as a kid, going in a boat at night added to the fun." (Photo: From the collection of Joseph Delorenzo)

The end of March, the beginning of April we'd work right up until Decoration Day doing all the things we weren't able to do in the fall to get prepared to open up for Decoration Day. But the hundred days was from early morning until midnight. We used to close at midnight.

We were one of the originators here at Bertrand Island Park of what we called "Nickel Night." All of our rides for years and years were a nickel on those nights. Of course, on those nights we attracted thousands and thousands of people. The parking lots were packed and people used to park all over the streets. The man that had the park before had one "Nickel Night" a week. When I came in there, we built it up so big, that we had to have two. He had it on Mondays. I had it on Mondays and Thursdays. Those two nights were packed all the time from the day we opened until the day we closed. That was strictly the rides that were a nickel. Everything else was the same price. The intent was not doubling the business so much as to make up the business. What it was, the rides were the attraction to get people into the park. The rides would bring in people at five cents, they were still spending twenty cents for a hot dog or twenty-five cents for a hamburger and ten cents to play the fish pond and ten cents to play the mouse game or ten cents to play something else.

That's for the first twenty years or so. Then we started calling them "Bargain Nights" because you couldn't give many more rides for a nickel anymore. The arcade was where all the machines were. Of course, years ago we called it the penny arcade. Then it changed to the arcade because there weren't too many pennies to do. Then, of course, things changed to a nickel in the arcade, and then they went to ten cents, and finally toward the last few years that I was down there, everything was almost a quarter. Every machine you wanted to play, you had to put a quarter in. There was still a few left at ten cents or a couple left at a nickel. Maybe one machine was still a penny just to have it there. But just like anything else, the way inflation took over, we went from "Nickel Night" to "Bargain Night."

We found that the fathers and mothers, oh by the hundreds, used to come to the park, drop their kids off right at the entrance to the park. They would have loads of kids in the car. Sometimes, they weren't just theirs, they could be half a

dozen kids they picked up around. Sometimes, I'd be standing out in the front and I'd hear them say, "Now don't forget, ten o'clock, we're going to pick you up right here." And
they'd give the kid two dollars or five dollars and that kid
with that two dollars or five dollars or whatever he had, he'd
run on the rides, he'd run on the rides, and, as soon as he
got finished with whatever rides, then the rest of the money,
he would spend on the stands. And, of course, I would say
that 99 and $\%_{10}$ percent of the kids, didn't have two cents or
five cents or ten cents left in their pocket when they left the
park. They had a good time. They were there to spend whatever they got and they just had a good time doing it.

Another confirmation of the long hours involved in the
amusement industry comes from Albert Reid, co-owner of
Keansburg Amusement Park in Keansburg, New Jersey. We also
see here an Horatio Alger success story.

I got out of college and I needed a new car. But I had a
home and I had other payments and things so I looked for a
part time job. I had relatives in this business and they said,
"Why don't you come in this business," and I said, "Well,
maybe, I don't know." I had five hundred bucks saved and I
borrowed five hundred from my father and I did go into the
business. I was running a wheel, a game of chance. We gave
out hams and turkeys and baskets of groceries to lovely
housewives and older ladies who would come down and
play a dime to win a pound of coffee or a turkey or something.

I did extremely well. I ended up eventually getting two
stands, and then a third one. Then, I bought that building
over there. I worked hard and saved my money. From that I
bought this park. The opportunity came to buy this place
with another gentleman. Together we pooled our resources
and bought this place.

From the last week in February through June, we work
seven days a week about eight to ten hours a day. Sometimes twelve. It's like this. You've got to understand it isn't
just administrative. There's a lot on spare parts. There's a
lot on hiring and firing and promotion and advertising that
is planned and instituted at that time. But the things that
really get you are, or let me put it this way — I've often de-

scribed running an amusement park as akin to being a damage control officer on a destroyer in the Philippines, say during the attack on Okinawa when the Kamikazes were attacking. We would be up here doing something very important, negotiating an insurance contract or something like that, and a call comes up: "Such and such a ride is down." There's people in the park and you don't want it down, so you say, "Okay, I'll get on that now. Tell the mechanic to meet me." Because no one knows the rides like we know 'em. Even though you've got mechanics, you've got to say, "Do this part here, not that." Every ride, I know. I have good hands and I can do things like that. I could be a mechanic. I'm not, but I fix stuff myself that some of the mechanics we hire don't know where to go for the problem.

I love very much the spring. I try to get out and paint a ride now and then myself. We've got a caterpillar ride down the end that I painted two years ago. I'd come in here and do the mail and do things in the morning real fast, then I'd start sneaking out one o'clock with a little work kit of paints and brushes and stuff. It's a little art work in itself. You can't let a stranger or a kid do it. I just loved it. It was the nicest time I spent. You get the sun and you sit there on a milk crate. You outline and you have your colors and it's marvelous. It's marvelous and it's a good break from the office. This is the hardest job here.

We had a woman come down here last summer, and it was a slow day toward the end of August, on a Monday. She brought her kids down from Holmdel, two kids to go in the water slide. And our help didn't show up that day and we were short all around. That's a slow day for the slide — it should open at eleven o'clock — so here it is twelve-thirty and we're not open. So, I got a call upstairs. "Boy, I'm catching hell down here. This woman is upset." I said, "What's she upset about?" "Well, she brought her kid down, and she promised the kid and she wants to go on this ride." So I thought for a second and said, "Tell her to go over to the ride and I'll be there in five minutes." I just put my stuff down and said, "That's it." I got a lifeguard whistle in here and I put it around my neck. I went over to the pool. I opened it up. I put the pumps on and I went over and introduced myself. Shook her hand and said, "I want you to know you're too valuable to turn down," I said, "I'm the boss and I'm here to take care of you personally, and if I don't do you good, you let me know." Well, gee, I enjoyed talking to them all afternoon. Another friend of hers was coming down too, and she came down later. They had three kids. And the place started to do a good business. I was there for two hours, and then we finally found somebody. But I left that person with, "I'm glad you shook me out of my lethargy and I was happy to do it, because you're the most valuable thing we've got, one customer, and there ain't nobody else I'm here for." It made my day, and it made her day, and her kids were happy. And by two o'clock, I had a few hundred dollars in there because other people came in and it was going good. And what more do you want. I get excited thinking about it. It's a great feeling.

Two things are. One, when you're fixing the equipment up, painting it, and it's spring and you've got it all sitting, shining and beautiful, well lubricated and tightened up and it's running quiet and it's pretty. Some people might collect stamps or vases or whatnot. To me this is a piece that's beautiful. It's something to be cherished. And the other thing is when you see the excitement. There's an electric excitement that is outside in the park. It's like in the wintertime when you close your car door and you get a shock. In a milder form, that's what it's like out there. This action. People are having fun. You're making money. There's excitement. There's attractive young people. There's all kinds of things happening. There's interaction. It's almost like life is happening ten times faster. That's what it's about. In fact you can't take too much of that. You burn out. But when it's happening, it's marvelous. There's a great satisfaction. We wrap up the week and get all the advertising in and get the help lined up and get the rides right, and all of a sudden you're ready to go home Saturday afternoon about four o'clock, "There's no brakes on the roller plane, or the chain broke or there's this terrible screeching noise." And you go out and the mechanic is gone. So you grab the tools and you go out. You listen to it. You look. You think. Maybe you grab your book and you look at these exploded diagram of parts. And you start and you say, "Okay, here's what we're going to do," and bing, bang, bing, and all of a sudden in forty-five minutes that thing is humming sweet. And you go home and you say, "That's good."

Robert Bennett of Seaside Heights, New Jersey, is another success story. Although, he eventually ended up owning not only a merry-go-round, but also an entire Amusement Pier, the early years were difficult.

I had started working here at the Casino Pier in probably 1949. I was doing different jobs here, operating rides, cleaning the swimming pool, working on the concession stands. When I came out of the navy, in 1956, then I opened my first concessions on my own, which were game concessions. That was the year that the state of New Jersey, through some technicality, closed all the games in the state. They found an old law, something on the books, that said that any person that wagers money against a prize is gambling, and gambling is illegal. It got so out of hand that they even made us take the brass ring off the merry-go-round because they said that people that paid to go on the merry-go-round were actually gambling that they were going to get the brass ring for a free ride. That was a prize and that was illegal too.

When they closed all of the concessions, I went to Cuba that year. I went to a park in Cuba called Coney Island Park in Havana, and what they had was Coney Island Road Shows. It was like a carnival that traveled around Cuba. And that was when the revolution broke out. So I went from my first year in business to the legislature closing the games down here in Seaside to a revolution in Cuba so my first couple of years in business weren't too rewarding. But, I kinda liked the business.

When I came back here to Seaside after Cuba, a lot of the concessionaires that were here for years and years and years had moved out because of the law. They just gave up and moved on. As a result, I was young and ambitious, and as they were moving out, the landlord that was here at the time said to me, "Bobby, open those places. I don't care what you put in." So, I was opening the places and putting anything in. One week they'd say, "This is legal, you can do that." And the next week, it was something else, but I kept making the changes just to keep the places open.

The atmosphere was horrible. In fact, there were so many of the motel owners and people who owned little cottages around town that were complaining because a lot of the people that actually came down here came for the atmosphere. The bingos and things like that that people used to enjoy playing. Skee ball alleys and the penny arcades where they would receive tickets or prizes. Well, without any of the atmosphere at all, the people weren't too happy without it. The people wanted it. When it was put up for a vote on a referendum, they spoke out and said they wanted it. The people in the state of New Jersey voted for the boardwalk games. Since then it's been legal. In 1958, when they legalized the games, I had a lot of locations on the boardwalk that I wouldn't have normally had, if it hadn't been for that law. That law actually was of benefit to me.

I was renting them at the time. For a long period of time that I was a concessionaire here, I always felt that I wanted to own something on the boardwalk of my own. I thought that maybe, possibly, one day, they might decide that maybe they wanted to sell the place. And if they wanted to sell it, maybe the guy that bought it might say, "Hey, Bobby Bennett, we want to operate these places ourselves. We don't need you anymore." That was probably my biggest fear.

Then in 1978, I bought a block of property in the middle of the boardwalk that's called the Coin Castle. It's an arcade and games. I was happy at that point because I just felt all these years just being a concessionaire, you never know really from day to day what could happen. When I bought that, I felt probably that I had a little more roots. In other words, I was into something that I owned now and as long as I wanted to be here, I could be here.

There's a lot of people I guess — and thank God, I'm not one of them — that catch the commuter train from Greenwich, Connecticut, and go into New York City and work all day long. Then have to run and catch the commuter train back at night. He does that fifty weeks out of the year. He takes his two weeks vacation and he goes away to play golf or whatever he does. Or he plays golf on weekends and can't wait for the day to come that he can retire and play golf.

Well, in my business, I work very hard, but I don't ever want to retire. I never considered getting out of the business. I just always felt that I wanted to stay in the business and I wanted to just keep it dancing. I don't ever want to retire. I love the business. In the summer months, I have to be here day and night, day and night. If it's eight in the morn-

Figure 35. Although Bob Bennett's merry-go-round, the historic Floyd L. Moreland Carousel, is a "menagerie" with several different animals, the horses are the preferred choice of most riders. (Photo: Dr. Norma B. Menghetti)

ing till two in the morning, it doesn't make any difference. I've been here at the Casino Pier — outside of my four years in the navy — and even the four years in the navy, I never missed the month of July. I was always able to get my leave. I was on a ship that went around the world two and a half times, but somehow, I was always here for the month of July. Like I said, since 1948, I've been here. That's over forty years, and I tell everybody the same story. I get up in the morning and never even have a cup of coffee at home. I run out of the house and I can't wait to get here every morning. I stop at Seven-Eleven and pick up a container of coffee and bring it up here and start going through some of my paper work. I love every minute of it.

One of the striking things revealed in the interviews is the joy these people in the amusement industry took in their work. Not one of the interviewees had anything but good to say about the industry. Along with the happiness they found in doing work they enjoyed was the other element of pride. All put in long hours and much hard physical labor, yet they obviously delighted in doing the very best job they could and were proud of their work.

4

The Biggest Problem We Have

As much as the people involved in the amusement industry enjoyed their work, the problems they encountered were enormous. Weather was a constant concern. Damage from fires, storms, and the public brought an end to many merry-go-rounds. The Great Depression and the Second World War were national events that affected individual owners and many parks. The common strand of difficulties shared by the narrators who took part in the Carousel Keepers Project verifies that although most felt their's was a good life, it was often a hard life. As Raymond D'Agostino tells us, the most feared adversary was the weather.

Rain. That's the only thing that would cause a bad season. If you were waiting for your weekend or you were waiting for the Fourth of July or you were waiting for Decoration Day or anything, and you had a rainy day, naturally nobody would come out. If we had a day where we were going to have forty or fifty busloads of kids and it started to rain, it was just unfortunate. Then the whole fifty busloads of kids wouldn't come up. Maybe ten or fifteen would show up because they couldn't book another day. They couldn't do very much because in the rain, what can you do in an amusement park? You can't ride the roller coaster. You can't ride most of the rides. You used to see some kids when they left the park, they were like drowned rats. Running around all day long in the rain. But what could you do?

It is unlikely that we will ever have a complete record of merry-go-rounds that were destroyed by fires or floods. Machines would simply be replaced, or if the destruction was not complete, other figures would be substituted for damaged animals. Owners often kept a few replacement animals on hand for just this purpose. Many of the "mixed" machines listed in the National Carousel Association Census originated when fires or natural disasters partially destroyed original carousels. Scott Bittler discusses the damage of floods at Eldridge Park, Elmira, New York.

Figure 36. Tragically, the beautiful PTC #36 merry-go-round at Seabreeze Park, Rochester, New York, was destroyed by fire in the spring of 1994. Only four horses that had been removed for restoration survived. (Photo: Courtesy Merrick Price)

In Eldridge Park, the two events that were of a destructive nature to the park were the two floods that occurred. There was the flood of 1956, and again another flood in 1972. All of the rain caused us very severe flooding. I forget how many feet high the flood level was throughout the park.

What they would do when they saw these things coming was raise the horses on the poles of the ride as high as they could and prop them up with wooden poles. Of course, they could do this for all the standers, but not for the jumping horses. For the jumping horses, they pretty much would put them at the even level, the mid point in their stroke and raise all the standers. It was too impractical to take them all off the ride and try to move them to higher ground. There was a hundred things to do. Also, at that time, you didn't get a whole lot of warning as you do today.

I remember mud, inches thick everywhere. The flood level was roughly on the order of six feet high in the area of the merry-go-round, I believe. Very much of the park was destroyed. The ticket box for the merry-go-round, a small wooden structure, was found after the flood out in the far portion of the roller coaster. The rides sustained a lot of damage that we basically had to take a season to recover from. A lot of wood joint separations and so forth that the ride simply had to be restored practically from scratch.

Rain was a problem, but if you were on a beach location, too much sun could also be a difficulty. The following excerpt from Edward Lange concerning the Palace Amusements in Asbury Park, New Jersey, presents a different weather concern, as well as other problems.

If the weather was good, we had a good season. If you had four or five rainy weekends, it hurt in the pocketbook. We made less, we didn't lose. But if you had a good season, not too hot, not too cold, and not too much rain, it was fine. Some people used to say when we had a real hot summer, "Boy, you must have had tremendous business." No. Too hot is no good. The people are on the beach all day. You can't compete with the sea. That's the main attraction. That's what people come here for, the sea. For the beach mainly. That's the main thing. The boardwalk and the beach. If you're on the beach all day in terrible heat, at night you don't have any energy. So the worst thing for us was extreme heat. When it would go up to ninety-five, forget it. You're dead.

We had a fire on the merry-go-round in the Palace. We had a fire in 1942. We were painting the horses. We were removing the paint, as we were going to do a real top notch job. Remove the paint and start all fresh. And, of course, we were using paint remover, and somebody lit a cigarette. Whshoosh! Thank God, the fire department came very quickly so only one section got burned. But fourteen horses were burned beyond redemption. So, we bought some horses up in New England. In Revere Beach, I believe.

We didn't have any policemen or anything. Until 1970. The riots. That was the peak. From there on, it was a slide. The thing is Asbury Park deteriorated. Very much. When I first came here, Asbury Park was a prime resort. First there was Atlantic City, number one, and Asbury Park, number two. I'm talking about fifty, sixty years ago.

Vandalism became a problem. 1970. We hired off-duty policemen. This was also another big expense. But you had to do it. We had burglar alarms, but we had one problem. The Ferris wheel went through the roof. Of course the ceiling was quite high. It was twenty feet. But the Ferris wheel was sixty feet. And of course there's a hole in the roof. You can't close the hole in the roof. They used to climb up on the roof, and then climb down the Ferris wheel, the framework and get inside. We installed all kinds of burglar alarms. Even radar. The movement of a person would set it off. But they learned after awhile, to not move fast and to get around the alarms. They could see the cameras. They used to break into

Figure 37. View of Wesley Lake, Asbury Park, New Jersey, showing the swan boat and the Ferris wheel going through the roof of the Palace Amusements. (Photo: From the collection of Edward Lange)

my office. Of course the safe was wired so they didn't get to the safe. But there was always change around and they took out bags of quarters. Oh, about three thousand or four thousand dollars.

Sometimes the alarm would sound. If they made one false move, then the alarm would ring. One time the sound didn't ring. It rang in the police station. We were hooked up to the police station. So, they didn't know it. The police came. The burglars saw the police trying to get in, and they got away because they climbed up the Ferris wheel over the roof. By the time the police called me up, and by the time we got down there and opened the doors, they were gone. But one was caught because, very stupidly, he went down two or three weeks later to a used car lot and bought a car with a lot of change. Stupid. So he was caught. He got put in jail for a couple years. Then one day, I was on the floor in the Palace and a young man came up to me and said, "Mr. Lange, how are you?" I said, "Fine, who are you?" "Oh," he said, "I'm the guy that robbed you two years ago." We became friends. Why not? Better be friends than enemies.

The fire that destroyed fourteen horses on the merry-go-round at the Palace was certainly bad. But a worse disaster occurred in Seaside Heights, New Jersey, when the carousel there was totally obliterated. As Dell Hopson reports:

When I came out the front door when the alarm went off, a northeast wind was blowing and it was raining like you wouldn't believe. I looked straight ahead and there was the [merry-go-round] building burning. It started from the neon sign and it lasted about four and a half or five hours. It started at four in the morning, and it burned the buildings right down to the ground. Even the pilings. But my father-in-law was a man of quick action and he had the bull dozers and the cranes and stuff in here that evening pulling all the debris out and getting ready to rebuild. We bought a smaller merry-go-round from Wildwood. We only had it one year. We were able to buy a merry-go-round from Coney Island the following year. I went up there and took the merry-go-round down and brought it down here and reassembled it in the building here. That's the present merry-go-round. An Illions. I believe it is now about one hundred years old.

Fortunately, such total destruction did not happen too often. More frequently, weather or fire damage, while severe, was not all-inclusive. A merry-go-round designed for travel used a canvas tent-like covering that presented its own potential for calamity during storms. Justin Van Vliet explains the difficulties with a portable carousel on the carnival circuit.

Figure 38. At age fifteen, Justin Van Vliet, Jr., was well established in the work routines of the traveling carnival. In this 1942 picture, he is shown attending a showman's convention at the Hotel Commodore in New York City. (Photo: Courtesy Justin Van Vliet)

One of the most disaster times we had that you can account in any carnival business was storms. Wind storms. When a wind storm came up, the first thing you did, you start the merry-go-round running. That's to keep the wind from getting underneath the top at any one place and tearing it to shreds. But if you got a good driving rain — these ran by gasoline powered engines — and if you got a good driving rain and the engine got wet and stalled, then you were in trouble 'cause the merry-go-round would stop and all the wind would billow just like a sail at one place. If it just tore the canvas, it was alright. But sometimes, it might tear the cornice out, stuff like that. At one time, we had to make a whole new cornice. That's what they call the rounding board. It outlined the frame. We had to build a new one from scratch. That was the worst fear.

When Hurricane Hugo was forecast to arrive in New Jersey during the summer of 1989, it presented a real threat to the amusement piers along the coast. Roy Gillian, at Ocean City, New Jersey, stressed the need for preparation in advance of the storm's arrival.

I worried about this past storm that came through, Hugo. In fact, we were at Dollywood in Tennessee, for a summer meeting. I left two days early to make sure that these things were all down. Then the storm went right around us and we really didn't get anything from it. But we were at least prepared. We prepare. This was the first year that I've had the big wheel. I was very worried about that. Although it's designed to stand a hundred mile an hour wind, it would certainly never take those two hundred mile an hour winds that came into Carolina. So these things are on your mind. We came back and we took all the canvas off the Himalaya, The Matterhorn. We sort of put the little canvas tops down over the Ferris wheel. We just tried to see how it was going to ride. Not much we can do on that. But that withstood, while it was in Florida, I think it went through a couple hurricanes down there without any problems. So hopefully. That's one of the unknowns. We have insurance on it, but I would hate to see any damage to it. We took all the rides downstairs, all that stuff was taken down and put up in here. Up in the building so that if we had high water, where it would come

Figure 39. Roy Gillian reports that the "Big Wheel" he purchased in Florida in 1989 is worth over two-hundred thousand dollars and cost fifty thousand to transport it to New Jersey. However, the wheel can be seen from the highway so it is good advertising for Gillian's Wonderland Pier. (Photo: Courtesy Roy Gillian)

into the lower end there, all that stuff was taken down and put up in here.

I've never had any real vandalism. We are so fortunate in this town. [Ocean City, New Jersey.] In all the years, the twenty-five years, I've never had a night watchman. We just have a super nice class of people that come here, and the people that live here year round. We are a tourist area. We go from a twenty thousand winter population, with ten thousand voters, up to about one-hundred-twenty-five thousand or one-hundred-fifty thousand during a weekend in the summer. I have really very seldom had problems.

At the Sanitarium Playground of New Jersey in Thorofare, Joseph Bornman observes that they too have had good luck regarding security of their Freidrich Heyn carousel.

Of course a lot of people who live here don't even know we're here. We don't do any advertising. This is not an amusement park open to the public. It's strictly for the benefit of the children, the under-privileged. It's been that way since 1877. Hasn't changed. The State wanted to help, but if you let the State in, they want to tell you how to run your operation. Forget the State. I don't want to hear it. They don't want nothing to do with the State. As of two years ago [1988] they started inspecting the carousel. It had never been inspected before. They found out we had a carousel. They start telling you how to run your operation right away.

How do you protect the carousel? I don't. God does. There's only so much that human ability can do. Just lock it. No alarms, but we have the police here constantly patrolling. Any strangers around here, they'd be picked up right away. At night time, when it's open in the summer, I leave the lights on all night. In the summertime, we take all those panels down and it's wide open. Then, I leave the lights on. It's very pretty to see it all lit up with the horses just standing still there. All so majestic, you know. They're white horses.

In addition to the weather affecting business, it also is an adversary of equipment. To combat damage from the weather, Albert Reid, co-owner of the amusement park in Keansburg, New Jersey, has a constant maintenance program of painting.

It's like the story of life. Life is a constant battle. You try and keep healthy and well as you progress through your life. And the rides are very much the same. You can scrape down one and paint it beautifully, new, shiny and crisp and it looks great. Then you go to the next and by the time you get to the last one, the first one needs to be painted again, and you just constantly revolve around. You keep going. And that's what the business is like mechanical wise.

Vandalism, oh now you're talking about a much greater adversary than the weather. We run into difficulties off and on through the spring and the fall when the park is open, but not occupied all week long. They will break bulbs and do bad things. There's always, it seems, somebody, somewhere, who gets their pleasure from ruining something. But we manage. We have watchmen out there, but sometimes it's like you take three steps forward and two back, and then another three forward and two back.

We have two or three uniformed officers. They are private security. And they keep things pretty well in order. I guess we have a rough and tumble history here. I don't know whether that has emanated out to you yet, but we're supposed to be a tough town and all that stuff. But now we've evolved much more into a mom and pop and two kids park. We took a survey out there and the most important reason why people come here are the kiddie rides. We've got two beautiful kiddie parks. They are all torn down now, you can't see them, but when they're open and painted up, they're beautiful. The kids love them. We still have several rides that were here in the 1930s. A little carousel over here. A little rocket ride. An airplane ride. Some of them are home-made. We've received many an offer from people who want to purchase or buy them from us.

[The merry-go-round and the horses,] that's indoors. They'd have been gone a long time ago. We had an arsonist who we refused a job to because he didn't look right. He felt

Figure 40. "Rodeo Ride" in Keansburg Amusement Park, Keansburg, New Jersey, is a miniature merry-go-round featured in Kiddieland. Kiddielands with small rides specifically made for children became a popular feature of amusement parks in the 1950s. (Photo: Courtesy Albert Reid)

that we were discriminatory towards him and he just burned us twice. Now he's in jail. An old farmer.

While narrator after narrator cited weather as the biggest worry in the amusement park industry, most felt the good days and the bad days averaged out. Like Robert Bennett, most of the narrators had developed a philosophical attitude towards the weather.

I've learned to accept, but I think my biggest problem would be to sit here on a Fourth of July weekend and see it pouring rain. Like I said, I've accepted because it's part of the business. There's so many things you can do things about, but there's nothing you can do about the weather. That's probably the most disheartening thing, to have everything all ready to go, and all the rides, the help is here, and you get a rainy weekend. Then, when you walk about the business, the concessionaires and the people are here, they all kinda have a frown on their face. It's so much nicer to walk around when business is booming and people are happy.

5

Honky-Tonk or Apple Pie

The role of amusement parks in the social history of our nation is a prominent one. How people spent their leisure time and what they did for entertainment was influenced primarily by the opportunities available and the amount of time and money people had to spend. As the industrial revolution transformed America from a rural agricultural society to an industrial and urban one, people had more leisure time and money than ever before. The rapidly growing middle and working classes wanted to participate in the life and fun of the seaside and mountain resorts that previously had catered mostly to the upper classes. Resort owners, trolley companies, and steamship lines saw the potential for expansion and offered transportation and day excursions to the new amusement parks that were evolving out of the genteel picnic groves and lake side resorts. Most parks featured a place for swimming and a few amusement attractions, and all were somewhat common, a little gaudy, and a bit sleazy. The noise and crowds, and the color and vibrancy of the honky-tonk atmosphere only added to the park's appeal. Although the more refined members of the Victorian public criticized the excitement and stimulation of the sensational attractions, the new middle and working class Americans loved them. Robert Bennett, owner of the Casino Pier in Seaside Heights, New Jersey, remembers his father's reaction to his entering the amusement industry.

Figure 41. The old postcard photo of the Endicott Johnson Boulevard Play Grounds in Johnson City, New York, shows how pleasantly a merry-go-round fits into a traditional park setting. (Photo: Ed Aswad, Carriage House Photography)

There was always a lot of satisfaction in the business. I don't think that I've ever regretted going in the business. My father was in the construction business, and when I was young, he kinda wanted me to follow in his footsteps and go into the construction business. But, I got a little taste of the boardwalk and I kinda liked it. He used to say to me "What do you want to be in that honky-tonk business for?" But, I think, that before my father died he realized that I was doing something that I enjoy. And that I was successful in what I was doing. I don't think he ever had any bad feeling that I didn't go into the construction business. I certainly don't.

I think there's always kind of a mystique about our business. We're always affiliated with the traveling carnival, that we're not people that are stable. I think that's only because people don't take the time to get to know us. In a town like Seaside Heights, there's got to be one-hundred-fifty individual business people here. I would say if there's one-hundred-fifty business people here, there's over a hundred of them that's family operated. The mother, the father and the children work in the business with them. And the majority of them probably live in this area, Ocean County. Don't forget when my father said this, it was forty years ago. I'm sure

90

that over the years, resorts, especially big amusement parks and things like that, people realize that it's a business, and it's like any other business.

The idea that there is something cheap and common about the amusement park is a belief that has not been entirely dispelled even today. Convincing people that there is little connection between a grand old carousel and anything honky-tonk was not always possible, as Charlotte Dinger discovered in Saratoga Springs, New York.

In Saratoga Springs, citizens raised money to preserve a carousel which they had hoped to put in Congress Park. Congress Park is a very elegant park with a lovely casino building. The people in the town, when it came right down to putting it there said, "We don't want a *carny* ride in Congress Park." What they didn't realize was that in the old days very elegant structures housed these lovely carousels. And they weren't painted in a gaudy way. They could be very elegant and very lovely. And with the little twinkling lights it could have been a lovely addition to the park. But they saw it as a *carny* ride.

I helped raise money to preserve that carousel by having an exhibition in the Casino building. I also gave a lecture there because I felt it was nice that the town was getting together and trying to preserve their carousel. And I thought that Congress Park was the perfect spot. But, they ran into town opposition. They had quite a different vision and trying to convince them just didn't work.

I remember reading about Colonel Parker who had a carousel factory in Kansas. He was referred to by the townspeople as *carny* folk, and that put him down a level socially. Even though, he had a lot of money and a big grand home, he was never accepted for that reason.

I enjoy carnival people. They usually travel with a number of rides. Some of them are con artists. You sometimes feel you have to hang onto your wallet when you speak to them because you can't believe what they say. That maybe reflects the carnival atmosphere. You know, the shill games and all the hype. But then there are some who are very sophisticated and honest business people, who know exactly what they are doing. So it's a whole broad spectrum. I don't think you can classify them in any one way.

Sometimes, respectability was determined by location. What might be considered disreputable in the culturally sophisticated cities of the East could take on a different flavor in the small towns of the West. Sol Abrams, press agent for Palisades Amusement Park indicates the difference.

> Have you traveled to amusement parks outside this area? Well, I have to tell you that outside the area, it's not like New York. I'm not talking about the Six Flags operation. That's a big corporate thing. But the smaller parks. Years ago. The wives played a very prominent part in the park operation. If they weren't active on the scene, they active on the social scene. They were very prominent people in the area. Not so much here with Palisades, but when you went out of the area to Rhode Island, or in Texas. That was a big thing

Figure 42. Since the elaborate Palisades Park Carousel PTC #84 originally was made for an amusement park in Vancouver, British Columbia, it is fitting that PTC #84 returned to Canada's Wonderland, Toronto, Ontario, in 1984. One of the last carousels built by the Philadelphia Toboggan Company, it is a four row carousel with sixty-four horses and two chariots. (Photo: Courtesy Richard Scheiss)

out there. They would also be involved in community activities, in the smaller towns. People would be looking up to them like they would the wives of a banker. Outside the big city areas. In the big city areas it was equated with being a business operation. But in the smaller towns, they were very prestigious people. Like this man I mentioned, Dr. Firestone. He was a dentist who fell in love with the amusement park. You found a lot of people that went into the park business that were very prestigious people in the area like the bankers, the merchants, the lawyers. People looked up to them.

They are not honky-tonks. Most people make the mistake of calling them carnivals or fairs. In the structure, at the top of the list is amusement parks, then come the fairs, then comes the carnival. If you would ever call an amusement park operator a *carny*, it's the worst insult that anybody can give or insult anybody with.

Over and over again, narrators pointed out that whatever previous ideas were about amusement park operations, those beliefs changed with the rise of Disney and the new theme parks of the 1950s. Owned by large and respected corporations, the theme park no longer was thought to be a small honky-tonk affair, but rather big business with all of the money, power, and esteem that implied. Roy Gillian, who owns one of the two remaining historic carousels in New Jersey, explains.

When you go visit other people's places, secretly you're always comparing. There's no doubt about it, we've got a lot of examples now to look up to. I think Disney started it all. Then the Six Flags and the Busch organization with all the money they have behind them. They have really made our industry something to be very proud of. Back in the old days, when my father started, they used to look down on people in this business. They were always a bunch of carnies or Gypsies or whatever. A lot of times these carnivals that would go around would have a lot of games on them. They were out to scam the people. I'm sure a lot of that has been cleaned up now, and I think that's good. Now I think we're looked upon as a very respectable type business.

I guess it [Gillian's Wonderland Pier in Ocean City, New Jersey] didn't do too bad because I was elected to be mayor

Figure 43. The public's perception of amusement parks changed with the advent of the great theme parks in the 1950s. Nearly all of the narrators credited the theme parks, especially the Walt Disney World Company, with bringing respectability, money and prestige to the amusement industry. Here. guests ride on "Cinderella's Golden Carousel" at Walt Disney World, 1988. (Photo: Courtesy Walt Disney World Company)

Figure 44. The bright lights, the music and the ring machine on the PTC #75 carousel at Gillian's Wonderland Pier in Ocean City, New Jersey, always draw a crowd. (Photo: Courtesy Roy Gillian)

of my own town here so that had to say something for it. Politics has always been part time for me. I've never let it interfere with my business. But, we're only busy in the summertime and I do have all winter that I have the time to give to the city. I've been in public office about eighteen out of the last twenty-five years. I'm in my fourth year now as mayor.

I'll tell you, we've just got a beautiful little town here. I'm very proud of it. I've been part of it my whole life so it's been good to me. As with my business here, I've always tried to run it and keep it up to date and make it look presentable. I'm proud of it in the summertime when people walk around here, it's well cared for. This is something that is part of a tourist area, or a vacation place. The kids just love it. There's no doubt about it that families that come to Ocean City, a lot of it is because they go to the boardwalk and ride the rides. That's part of a vacation.

Mr. Edward Lange in Asbury Park, New Jersey, saw the perception of the amusement industry change from being considered a somewhat inferior venture to being thought of as a a highly respectable business. He too, believes the theme parks must be credited with the transformation.

The amusement business became more acceptable, I think, because of the parks and the Disneys. Great Adventure was built. It became more recognized. In the beginning, when you said amusement, right away people thought carnival. Right away it was carnival. But, I would tell them, "No, this isn't a carnival. This is a permanent place." A carnival moves from one town to another like Gypsies.

In the early days, [social status] might have been a problem. I didn't have too much time to socialize anyway, so I wouldn't recognize if there was a little opposition or no acceptance. I know a lot of people in the beginning tied it up with carnival, which wasn't so. Later on, I became involved in activities, in civic affairs, and in the Presbyterian church. I became a trustee. I wasn't only a follower, I became president of the United Fund. In the Lion's Club, I was president. When I was man of the year, everybody thought very highly of me. To me, Asbury Park was my life and my fu-

Figure 45. Today the Palace building in Asbury Park, New Jersey, is slated for demolition to make room for beach front development. The original Palace building, with its antique Ferris wheel going through the roof, was built in 1888 by Bethlehem Steel. It was one of the first indoor amusement parks in the United States. (Photo: Carrie Papa)

ture. I was a business owner. I was happy. We were the main amusement attraction in Asbury Park. The Palace. And, of course, the Casino was next. Between the Palace and the Casino, that was it. When I came to Asbury Park in 1926, it was a prime resort. First there was Atlantic City, number one, and Asbury Park, number two. It was great. Year after year, we improved. We doubled the size of the Palace. We bought properties adjacent and we made it twice as big.

Not everyone felt the Disney Worlds, the Busch Gardens, or the Six Flags were the best thing that could have happened to the amusement industry. At Keansburg Amusement Park, Keansburg, New Jersey, owner Albert Reid firmly believes a lot was lost when the theme empires replaced the individually owned family parks.

We've evolved into a mom and pop and two kids park. Today, Six Flags goes out and builds a multi-million dollar park. But, I don't really think we get a tremendous amount of competition. We have sort of an apple pie kind of park here. We don't have too many exotic things. This is a mom and pop blue collar place. You come and spend the day and you don't have to spend a lot of money. We have an over abundance of kiddie rides. Great Adventure doesn't have that. We have the most kiddie rides of any park in the states. They are all torn down now, but when they're open and painted up, they're beautiful. The kids love them. We have rides that were here in the 1930s. A little rocket ride. An airplane ride. Some of them are homemade. We've received many an offer from people who want to purchase or buy them from us. A little carousel. It's made by a company called Mangles, which now is out of business. It's not a wooden horse. It's made for outdoor use. It's a cast horse. But it's a

Figure 46. In the 1990s, Keansburg Amusement Park continues to direct its advertising to Mom and Pop. With reduced prices on food, some free rides, and fireworks, Keansburg is justified in billing itself as "loads of fun." (Photo: Carrie Papa)

nice little carousel. Kids love it. We're all jammed in close. You don't walk four hundred yards to get to another ride like you do in Great Adventure.

Each park, each amusement park, has it's own personality, but the new ones, the big ones, the rich ones, I really would just call them plastic places. That's really what they are. It's a commercial product. It's the golden arches of McDonalds.

I'm trying to show you the difference between this type of operation and Great Adventure. I don't want to pick on them — they have enough troubles — but they use frozen fries in Great Adventure, and they stamp out a McDonald's hamburger. This is different here. Our food far exceeds most. What we put out is good. You have to be here to get the flavor of it, the smells and the noises and the kids excitedness. They're off one ride and running for the next ride. And Mom wants to go play a game and win a toaster or something like that. And somebody else is playing for a box of candy. Then the teenagers want to throw a ball at the milk bottles. That kind of thing. It's constant. It's wall to wall excitement when it's going.

We don't charge admission. Wherever they can park, they park and come right in. You can bring five bucks and have a hell of a day. When the spring starts, people stream out and they want to get on those rides. We get calls, "Are you open?" "Are you open?" "Is it okay to come down?" "What time?" That's a nice feeling. And, in the spring you leave your windows open and it's nice. You hear a saw going out there. You hear somebody hammering. And the activity starts and you know we're coming back to life like a flower starting to bloom.

And was life on the carnival circuit really so disreputable? Perhaps we can get a good idea of the actual social status of carnival folk from Justin Van Vliet, who grew up with the B & V Shows and spent his life traveling with his parents on the carnival circuit.

My father and mother were both in the carnival business. We used to move from town to town mostly by truck. The whole family was out on the road together. The traveling carnival started the original RV's [Recreational Vehicles]. On the truck shows, they had house trailers, and some people took load vans and made homes out of them. We had one concessionaire, he had three concessions. In the back part, he used to store his concessions and his merchandise and in the front part, he had living quarters. It was just as nice. Had a rug on the floor, a little bedroom, a little kitchenette, a little settin' room. It was a thirty-two-foot trailer.

Myself and my brother, we lived in a tent, and we used to leave our stuff laying around and never had nothing stolen. The same with the trucks. We used to leave the trucks open. Never nothing stolen. Nowadays, you would have everything under lock and key. But, in those days, we used to just leave everything set. Just like you were all neighbors, one big family. If you had problems, one helped the other.

My sister, she used to work what was known as a "pan". We called it a pan. Muffin pans, you know, painted different colors. They played different odds. The ball would roll down the different odds, whatever the odds you had, a quarter, a dime on it, and you got whatever the odds were, like ten to

Figure 47. Wherever the carnival set up, the merry-go-round was always one of the most popular rides. This old merry-go-round ran on a track driven by a cable. (Photo: Courtesy Justin Van Vliet)

one, five to one. Somehow or other the table got knocked, and it wasn't perfectly level. So the ball would ride to seventy-five to one. My brother, he almost had my sister in tears. They couldn't set the thing right. They knew something must be wrong, but they had to keep playing like that. Kept going back to my brother for a bankroll to keep paying it. Good thing, we were in a town where she knew some people who kept supplying them with dimes and quarters. Naturally, once we closed down that night, we fixed it. But, what happened here, it had rained all the prior week, and just one spot, one leg on the table sank in the ground. That's how those things happen. Most of your concessionaires, they were strictly on the up and up.

The good old days. When you move from place to place, like from one town to the other, you had people waiting there for you. When we got ready to start setting up, we had people waiting to go to work. We had people follow us from place to place. They knew what to do. You didn't have to tell them, "We gotta do this, you gotta do that." They did it. Up in Pennsylvania, you'd have a waiting list. People who wanted to get a temporary job during the Depression. More or less, like I said, we always had the same help. When we was up in the coal mines, I had the same crew. They used to come down in the middle of the week, "What time are we going to start Saturday night?" We used to tell by the town what time, "Oh, eleven-thirty." So about eleven-thirty, they'd be there with their work clothes on. It was good.

We had good working relations with the police, with the town, with the fire department. In fact, we had one town up in New York state, I think it was Cortland, New York, the fire department used to have a big doings every year. Well, the carnival spot that they used, they couldn't get no more because they were going to build a factory on it. So my father went up about two weeks before to look at the new lot and see it. He went down to the Fire Chief and says, "How am I going to get in that lot? There's no way to get in. There's a big gully all around." They had like a drainage ditch all around. "Oh, we never thought of that," he says, "don't worry about it. We'll have it taken care of by the time you get here in three weeks." So, we get there in three weeks, and here they built this bridge out of these big 12 by 12 timbers. The Fire Department — mostly everybody in the Fire

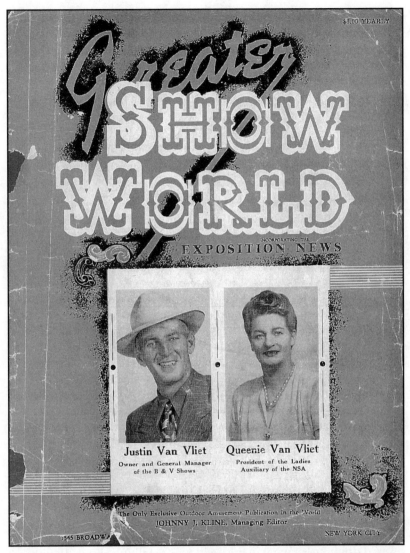

Figure 48. In 1948, Justin Van Vliet and his wife Queenie were featured on the February cover of *Greater Show World*. (Photo: Courtesy Justin Van Vliet)

Department was volunteers — so they built this bridge. No problem.

Most all the towns we played, we were accepted. We used to play for the firemen up in Newton, New Jersey. My father knew the man that owned the restaurant. I was up there one time — my father got tied up somewhere. And the men had to be fed. I didn't have the money to feed them. I had money, but not enough to feed fifteen-twenty men so I go down to the restaurant and I told the man. I can't think of his name, but I told him the story. He says, "No problem. Just tell them to come in. We'll take care of them."

Saturday night, most of the towns had ordinances that you couldn't have loud noises after a certain hour. Sometimes, they used to bend it. It was up to the local Chief of Police, more or less. My father got along good with all of them. Like, one time, they had a ten-thirty curfew, and the Chief of Police says, "Forget about it," he says, "I'm not going to be available."

Some of your towns, the Building Inspector had to come around. But most of the time, like putting up a merry-go-round or a Ferris wheel, the Inspector, he takes a look, "Well, what's this for? What's that for?" I had one come down one day, he says, "I've got to inspect, make sure you're doing it right." I said, "Alright." I'm not going to argue with the man. There were a couple people standing by when he said that, but they walked away. And, he says to me on the sly, he says, "I don't know the first damn thing about this. Do whatever you want," he says, "just as long's it's safe." "Well," I said, "we've been operating for years and we never had a Ferris wheel tip over or anything like that yet." So, he just walked away." I said, "come back when everything's up and I'll explain just what's what to you so you're covered." He says, "Okay." So, he comes back. We're operating two days when he came back. "I was tied up." "Yeah, I know." So, I took him around and showed him how we block things up and stuff like that. And he wrote a little thing and let me read it. He says, "Just initial that you read it." I said, "You did a better job than I expected you to." He says, "I did?" Like I was pinning a medal on him. He says, "To tell you the truth, I don't know what in the devil you're talking about" [laughter].

Most of your Police Departments, they checked when they came around. My aunt, the last year that she was on the road, she had a duck pond, her and her husband. They would have to take all the ducks and turn the face up to see that all the numbers correspond. The big prize, she only gave one, the smaller prizes, naturally she had more than enough. But she had at least one duck for every big prize, when she turned it

Figure 49. Part of Justin Van Vliet's responsibilities on the carnival circuit was to drive one of the "B & V Show's" fourteen trucks to the various locations. In addition to driving the truck, Justin helped move what in the carnival business was referred to as the "pig iron." That is, he set up and took down rides such as the Ferris wheel and chair plane that were mostly made up of iron. (Photo: Courtesy Justin Van Vliet)

Figure 50. Binghamton, New York, is proud of its carousel heritage. Horses from the six Broome County carousels are found on postcards, street signs, and other displays. (Photos: Edward Aswad, Carriage House Photography)

up. Not only her, but others. Like, with throwing hoops over the bar, 'cause some of these put smaller hoops that wouldn't fit. Everybody, no matter who they are, if they think they can get away with something. . . . But, all in all, with most of the Police Departments, we had a good thing. All the years I was up through the state of Pennsylvania, we never had no problems.

What I enjoyed about it, every week you had different scenery and there was always something doing. It was something to look forward to, and I've seen parts of the country that people I went to school with never see. I mean, wherever you went, you had different people from one town to the other. At fair time, our carnival used to swell from maybe about one-hundred-fifty to two hundred people, it might swell up to five hundred people. All working people and concessionaires. They were in business for themselves. We used to tear down on a Saturday night. Move to the next town. Set up generally on Sunday. Finish up on Monday.

We had our affairs. Almost every Wednesday night, we had what you call a jamboree. After the show closed, about eleven o'clock, we used to go into one of the bigger tents, where the girl's show would be or something like that, and we'd have a party. We had one guy, he bought a fiddle and he learned to play it. Another played the accordion. We used to have dances, stuff like that. All the carnival people themselves. That's including children. From babes in arms right up to older people. Just had like a little party. It was nice while it lasted. Like I say, I enjoyed it.

6

Buying and Selling

One of the most entertaining aspects of the Carousel Keepers Oral History Project is the many stories that were reported on buying and selling carousel figures or entire merry-go-rounds. With today's escalating prices for carousel figures and memorabilia in the antique market, the narrators were aware of either opportunities they had missed or fantastic deals they had made. Nearly everyone had some kind of horse tale to relate. Charlotte Dinger's was:

> I always had hoped someday, I'd have a carousel horse of my own. In 1972, long after Olympic Park closed and the carousel moved, I started to look for a horse to put in our home. I found a small primitive horse in an antique shop in Philadelphia and paid seventy-five dollars for it. It was not elaborate. I restored it, and I had it in our hall for a number of months. I kept looking at it and thinking, "I would love to get another one." Something more like the elaborate ones that I remembered at Olympic Park. So, I began my quest and I ended up finding twenty carousel horses in an antique dealer's garage in Pennsylvania, stacked like firewood, laying one on top of the other. They had been used to decorate a restaurant, I understand. I was very fortunate that I was able to track them down. It took a lot of phoning and detective work. I ended up buying all twenty. So, of course, I was an instant collector, and that started me on this hobby.

The animals were a mixture of all different carvers, which was very nice as that started me on a varied collection. I didn't know anything about them, but I knew they were very interesting and they were large and elaborate. Very nicely carved. And I recognized that they weren't all from the same carver because you could see that some animals had a very aggressive look, and some of them were sweet and gentle. I could see that there was a variety there, but I knew nothing about who had carved them.

I very much like the Muller Indian Pony in my living room. It's one of my favorites, and one of the favorites of collectors too. Many would put that at the top of their wish list, I think. I found him in a home that was owned by an elderly man who had an Indian museum many years ago. When the museum was disbanded, he brought all of the artifacts from the museum, which included jewelry, a war canoe, a buffalo's head and all sorts of things, to his home. I went to his home and remember having to climb over the canoe to get in the front door, and into the hall. It was just as if he had taken this huge museum and condensed it into his home. There was a little narrow path to walk through, there was so much stacked up close to the ceiling. It was incredible. And there was this horse. Of course, it had an Indian motif, and it was sitting by a window with a cat sitting on the saddle. I could not see anything except the upper portion from the chest up because there was so much stacked around it. And it was far away from me. I couldn't even get close to it. But I knew it had a wonderful head. It was very animated and had a wind blown mane. I just loved the look of the horse, so I bought it from him and didn't really see all of it until we moved all of the things out the next week. I brought it home and I was really amazed at how wonderful it was.

[The Stein & Goldstein,] I found it outside of Albany, New York. An antique dealer called me and said she had the greatest horse she'd ever seen. Well, I'd heard that before. But then, she described it. She said, "it's enormous, had old paint, and there are roses on it." Well then, of course, I thought I must go up immediately and see it, so I drove up in my station wagon the next day. It was a fabulous horse and I thought, "I must not let this stay here because it's something that will sell fast." So, I bought it right away. I couldn't fit it in my station wagon. It was much too large. So, I asked the dealer if she had a mattress or any kind of padding that I could put on the roof of the car. She had an old mattress so we strapped it on, and I drove down from Albany [to Morristown, New Jersey] with the horse on the roof. I'm so happy I found that exquisite animal. It's one of my finest horses. I collect because I love the animals. They have brought me a great deal of pleasure.

Today some people are just buying as an investment and not because they feel anything for the animals. That's a change that I've only seen in the last five years. [Since 1985.] So there's that factor. But that's because the prices have been driven up. They've been increasing steadily at a very fast

Figure 51. Sadly, Philadelphia Toboggan Company carousel #36, which had been installed at Seabreeze Park, Rochester, New York, in 1926, was destroyed by fire on March 31, 1994. Four horses that were undergoing restoration by grandaughter Susan Hofsass are all that remain of the 1915 carousel. Merrick Price, son-in-law of George Long, reports that a new carousel pavilion has already been built to house the new hand-carved wooden carousel they have commissioned. Four original horses were placed on the new carousel along with thirty-eight others that were carved by Ed Roth for the park. The new carousel opened June 1, 1996. (Photo: Courtesy Merrick Price)

rate. Before that, most of the people who collected just loved the animals.

The changing perception and value of carousels from just another amusement ride to being considered genuine folk art is evident from George Long, Jr.'s, account.

I was tied up in that carousel that sold at Roseland Park. That's thirty miles East of here at Canadaigua, [New York.] Bill Murer came to me in 1937 and said, "I want you to put a carousel in down there." So, I have a cousin, Tom Long, who bought and sold horses and carousels and he was pretty good. He was an Irishman. So, in 1937, Bill Murer said, "Why don't you put a carousel in down in my park?" That's the Roseland Park. I said, "Okay." So, I called my cousin Tom, and I said, "Tom, I've got a location for a merry-go-round. Do you want to sell me a carousel?" "Yup. I got just what you want." So, he brought it up here and I set it up and I operated it, oh, two or three years.

Then, I found a better carousel at Long Branch Park in Syracuse. The park had been discontinued. The place had been locked up. The tar paper blew off the roof. They had taken the horses off the machine and left the rest of the machine intact. I went down there and looked at it and the tar paper had blown off so the roof leaked water for I don't know how long. A couple of years probably, and the horses were laying in pieces. All over the place. So, I said. "You wanna sell it?" The man said, "Yes." I said, "I'll give you fifteen hundred dollars." He said, "I'll take it." That's all the conversation consisted of. I paid him the fifteen hundred dollars. We took the horses out and brought them to Seabreeze. I owned the hardware store at the time. We had a second floor room up there that we weren't using so I brought the horses there. Put them all back together again and repainted them. Took the rest of the machine to Canadaigua so as to have a bigger machine there. Put the horses in Roseland Park in Canadaigua with the machine.

In 1945, Bill Murer came to me and he said, "I'd like to buy that carousel." I was busy at Seabreeze. Seabreeze was improving all the time and I took the operational park over on a rental basis from the transit company. So we agreed on

108

a price of sixty-five hundred dollars, including the building I built there.

And that sold — take you off your pins — that sold last fall, a year ago this past fall [1985] for three-hundred-and-ninety-seven thousand dollars! Now compared to this machine at Seabreeze, those carvings — they're good carvings — but they don't have the detail that these horses have. They just don't have it.

Of course they're disappearing now. More and more carousels are being taken apart and being sold piece by piece. There are a lot of people in this carousel association that don't know the first thing about carousels. A few of them do, but they are all late comers because that's only been in existence about twelve years, and they just don't know about the operation of carousels.

I think it's been over done really. People have gone so crazy about wood carvings. The trouble is there are a few people who recognize good carvings, but there are a lot of people who don't know a good carving when they see it. Because they don't know enough about the details. And some of the carvings that people pay a lot of money for, that's just too bad because they're just hooked. But they'll do it.

Some of those horses are done by a very good carver. The heads especially. Now a lot of that work is done in all of these shops where they give a man — that's a professional carver — certain things. You work on the legs, and you'll work on the bodies up to a certain point. Then the good carver will come in and finish it up. But the good carver can see if a line is off, a line that doesn't have a proper curve. But people will buy them. Just because it was a merry-go-round horse. And some of the stuff is terrible. It pushes the market up, that's all.

Not all of the Trustees were happy with the decision of the Martha's Vineyard Preservation Trust to purchase the Flying Horses carousel. Although the merry-go-round had been on the Island since 1884, and is the oldest platform merry-go-round in the United States, many of the Trust's members were against the project. Jane Chittick, Executive Director of the Preservation Trust at the time, explains.

It was not in anyone's mind. In 1986, the then owner, James Ryan, who owned a string of amusement companies in the Cape Cod area and part of the Island, decided that he no longer wanted to own this carousel. He bought it about three years before, and didn't want to operate it either. So, he approached the Preservation Trust and asked if we had any interest in it. And that started a debate within the Trust, and, really, I would say the board was split. Some people thought that this was ridiculous for a preservation society. And what did we want with a merry-go-round. And others felt it was very important. I was part of the latter group, and thought it was extremely important. He was offering the carousel at a firm price of seven-hundred-and-fifty thousand dollars and the small amount of land on which it sits, the building and the carousel itself.

I had to make an arrangement with Mr. Ryan. That was, that we would operate the carousel that summer for him — he didn't want anything to do with the business of it — in return for giving us until December of 1986 to make a decision whether we could raise enough money to buy it or not.

Figure 52. The Flying Horses — consisting of twenty Charles Dare carvings, ten large outer horses paired with ten small inner horses — came to Martha's Vineyard in 1884 and have been at their present location since 1976. This carousel is a Registered National Historic Landmark. (Photo: Alison Shaw)

Certainly the expense, seven-hundred-and-fifty thousand dollars [was an objection]. For a child's toy, and a run-down one at that. Sort of a honky-tonk amusement park, sort of a Coney Island thing. "What will we do with it?" "What on earth does this have to do with historical preservation?" So, it took convincing them.

Later that year, although it was after the fund-raising, it was designated a National Historic Landmark. The government chooses you. Landmarks are entirely different than the National Register. It's the Senate and the House of Representatives and the Parks Department, Department of the Interior, and they decide. You can not apply for it. They simply decide what is going to be on it and what isn't. Usually, it follows a three to four year study period too. They knew it was the oldest one in the country. I think they were looking at carousels in general, and they selected — I think it was ten of them that are now National Historic Landmarks. And, we were considered the premier candidate for this designation because of its age. So when that was known, and made known, that convinced the remaining skeptics on the Board. Eventually, we were successful in convincing the Board to go ahead.

By December, we had raised five-hundred-and-forty thousand dollars of this seven-hundred-and-fifty thousand dollars. So, we made a decision at that point to borrow the remainder. We have a mortgage on the carousel. We reduce that each year. Our earnings go right back into the carousel.

Another instance of a government agency, this time the Smithsonian Institution, being an influence for good in convincing a group that a carousel is a worthwhile item to own happened with Washington Cathedral's All Hallows Guild. According to Jane Lee:

The purpose of All Hallows Guild is to raise funds and oversee the beautification of the Cathedral Close, which is fifty-seven acres. So that's their main thrust, and the carousel itself is incidental. Some of the people who voted for it occasionally will say, "Why don't we get rid of that and just rent one?" And, I say, "Cause you can't rent one. There are not any for rent." I was so determined because I was so con-

Figure 53. Each seatback of the sleighs on the All Hallows Guild carousel has a scene of a Washington momument in the medallion. All of the beautiful decorative painting was done by artists of the Nation's Capital Chapter of the National Society of Decorative Painters. (Photo: Karen Smith)

vinced myself that it would make a difference to the *Flower Mart*, and it has. I mean, right in the corner where it is.

I was asked to go on the Executive Committee, and I accepted quickly to protect my carousel. Now the first year we bought it, it was a great break for me. The Smithsonian did not have a carousel and they rented ours for what seemed to me the most enormous lot of money. So, this made me very happy. Here, the very first season we bought it, we made . . . . I don't know what they paid, but it seemed like an awful lot of money.

We're not going to sell it! As long as I live, it's not going to be sold. It's going to live up there forever.

After telling how his father purchased new aluminum horses for their Allan Hershell merry-go-round and threw the wooden horses away, Justin Van Vliet did recall that actually two horses had been saved.

We kept two of them. I don't know what become of the one. One, my uncle up in Kingston had it on his front lawn for years. His kids used to ride it. He used to keep it painted up, but then I don't know what became of that. I guess it just deteriorated being out in the weather. He had it on the front lawn. Never realized the value of them.

Even someone involved with carving could not know the future value of a carousel horse, or that merry-go-round figures would be placed in museums as fine examples of American folk art. Scott Bittler tells the following story about his grandfather, Mr. Robert Long, and the Eldridge Park carousel.

Figure 54. In the 1970s, Robert A. Long carved away the trappings on one of the magnificent lions on his carousel at Eldridge Park, Elmira, New York. The lion was then donated to the Lion's Club of Elmira to be used as a mascot. (Photos: R. Scott Bittler)

Back, gosh this was in the 1970s, I guess, one of the things my grandfather did was to donate one of the magnificent lions that he had to the Lion's Club in Elmira, New York as their mascot. Some people that knew of it were very upset with the fact that he carved away all of the trappings and made it look like a natural lion. He did that to make it more fitting as a mascot for the Lion's Club. Many of the early carousel enthusiasts, as I'll call them, were disgruntled with the fact that he did that. But, again, I think the reason, he did that was because it was not viewed with the artistic standpoint that they are today. Again, he was putting it out there for a use that was of a different mind set than people have today. As far as I know they still have it and still use it for that purpose. It's on a great big trailer and they pull it in their parades and things like that.

Trading in a small merry-go-round for a larger one, switching carousels from a machine with all stander figures to one with jumpers or updating an old carousel for the latest model was a common practice during the years when the merry-go-round was thought to be just another aspect of the amusement business. Roy Gillian recalls one mistake he made in trading merry-go-rounds.

The first one that I had was an old secondhand with stationary horses that we bought from Forest Park up in Pennsylvania. We brought it down and probably if we knew the value then what they are now, it was worth a fortune because it had fifty stationary animals on it. But nothing went up and down. I used it one year, and then traded it in for a portable King. Little carousel with plastic horses, but they went up and down.

I have no idea what it was. There was no way of ever telling at that point because it looked like a homemade deal, really. But it had the lions, giraffes. Nowadays, if that were in one piece, it would be worth more than mine down here. The animals on it were gorgeous.

I goofed. Sure. Back in those days, nobody looked at these things as being valuable.

If you were fortunate enough to have bought a carousel back in the days when prices were reasonable, you may have made an investment that skyrocketed in value. On the other hand, you may have purchased something that continues to drain your finances. National Carousel Association Conservation Chairman, Charles Walker, speaks of the merry-go-round he bought.

This machine originally had three rows of jumping horses and a row of outside standing horses. It's fifty-two feet across and was made in 1919–1920, and was installed in Central Park in Allentown, Pennsylvania. In the fifties it was moved from there because the park closed and there was a bad fire. In fact, this carousel almost burned up, had a lot of fire damage on it. One side of it had three sections that were charred pretty bad. Then some people in Tampa, Florida bought the carousel and took it to Tampa, and set it up with a tin roof on the ground. And, it operated down there to the sixties, and they were having integration problems, and they closed the park. For about five or six years, the carousel sat out in the weather. During that time period, the outside horses got wet because the tin roof wasn't sufficient, and all that moisture down there in Florida, they all came apart. Really, what I got basically was a pile of hardware, and I am reconstructing a carousel from that.

But, anyway, we got it delivered to my yard, and we stored it in the barn in Griffin. I got over forty-six original horses, and some of those were in bad repair. Some were coming apart because the place where it was stored was all wet so all the glue joints had come apart. Some of them were in bushel baskets and had to be glued back together. My father was so overcome by what he was seeing, all these horses strewn out on the lawn trying to get 'em straightened out before we stored them in the barn, he said it looked like the battle of Atlanta, with all these horse parts laying around all over the place.

Had no idea how much needed to be done to it until I got started. So, I decided that I was going to build a building somewhere, or find a building, to put this carousel together in to work on it. Not being able to find one that was sixty feet square with no posts in the middle, I had this idea to construct it in the back of my studio. But first, I had to buy the property, so I was forced into buying the land. No sooner had I bought the property, than all the developers came around and started saying, "We want to put a high rise building there, and we don't want you to build anything because we want to tear it all down and we want you to get out of there." I didn't pay any attention. I went right ahead and built this building just to work on the carousel. It's sixty feet square and had a thirty-five foot peak in the ceiling 'cause the center pole is about twenty-six feet tall.

Then we began to work on it, putting it together. When we first erected the center pole, we learned a lot. The pole got away from us and fell, and, of course, there was no problem with the people that were helping trying to find the exit doors of the building. We were sort of concerned about that when we built the building, but they got right out. So, that set us back a year because there was damage to the bull gear that went up in the center. But, we got that back together and then we started again. The big expense that I have now is to build a floor for it. The original floor rotted out years ago, and so they had these huge sheet metal plates for the floor. And, I'd like to go back to an original wood floor. I have plans for that, but that's an expense.

I would say that I probably have about twenty-five or thirty horses [restored.] But the horses don't take a whole lot of time. You can do that kind of thing in your basement. You don't have to have a sixty foot building to do that it. Now, I'm not as fussy as some of these people. Most of the people out there in the world have gotten to where they worship these things and they're like some great Gods that have come out of the past. If you take that kind of attitude, then there may not be enough hours in the day to get it in that kind of condition. But, I have to look at it from a business standpoint if I'm going to operate a carousel to make money, then, I want everything to be safe, but it doesn't have to be museum quality restoration.

When I talk to people who want horses for their homes or animals for their homes, it's like they were put off of a horse one time on a carousel, and they've never gotten over it. Now they want one for their very own in their house. It's a very strange thing. You run into ones who think that these are such great works of art and the crazy thing is that they were all done on a carving machine, on a duplicating machine. We're talking about people who were putting these things out in mass quantities. The original design for the heads of the horses, the style, the people who set the styles for these things, they did have artistry. But the originals, once they were carved and put on a duplicating machine, then they just knocked them out like chopping wood. The thing is, it's the stupidity of the public and the stupidity of the people who are coming on to think that these are one of a kind items. All you've got to do is look at the legs. The legs on them are all exactly the same. The heads, there may be three or four different styles, and the tails are all the same on most of the horses. The ones that are truly rare are the ones that were not done on the duplicating machine, and you'd have to find one that was made before about 1906 or 1907 in order to get one. There are very few of those left.

I think that one of these days, the value of the wood horse will probably diminish because the people who right now can relate to wood animals are headed for the cemetery fast and furious, and when they hit the cemetery, then the next generations probably will be able to relate to the bumper cars and the Pac Man machine more than they will the carousel horse, because there's less than one-hundred-eighty in the country with wood horses. It certainly is not a very good investment unless you really love it as much as you pay for it. I would just advise not putting my money into carousel horses unless it's on a machine where it can gather some revenue. I don't understand why these people that have money enough to have a carousel horse in their house, they've got enough money to own a whole carousel. What they ought to invest in is a whole machine. Then, they could have it up and they could have their cake and eat it too.

To me, the machine as a whole is so graceful because it's meant to all be together. It's sort of like tearing a house down and taking all the carved ornaments and the columns and everything and selling them off separately. The house looked beautiful when it was all together in one piece. The individual items are beautiful, but not as beautiful as the whole machine or the whole house together.

I have these brochures that I pass out at the International Association of Amusement Parks convention that sort of cheer people on who have old carousels. You have to concentrate on how you're going to get these people, how you're going to sell them on the idea that their antique carousel is the thing, and they should hold on to their heritage because that's the only weapon that we have against the auction companies who are encouraging everybody to sell off. They are saying, "Okay, you've got five-hundred thousand dollars to seven-hundred-fifty thousand dollars tied up in that carousel, and you could put that money on some flashy new ride." But, they don't seem to explain to the people that they have to replace the carousel too. You might find that you would spend as much on a new carousel, a new fiberglass carousel, as you would get out of selling off the old one, depending on who showed up for the auction. A lot of people who own these carousels are just being done in financially by the ploy of the auction companies, who are in business to sell.

We know of cases where they have absolutely pestered people into selling. The amusement park [people]. You see, those people are the ones who own the carousels. They're the keepers of the carousels currently. It's up to them whether they're wanting to sell them off or . . . . If you've got one together, it's kind of like melting down your silver service, the silver is worth something okay, but one day, the silver service will be worth a lot more because there won't be that many silver services.

I think right now the way the economy is today, I think it would be very risky to have an auction and sell off your carousel because you might find . . . . The past two or three have not brought near what they promised they would bring. When you see inside row horses going for fifteen hundred dollars and twelve hundred dollars apiece, then you know you're in bad trouble. The auction company is telling people that they can get three thousand dollars or four thousand dollars for an inside row animal. I think it's a dangerous thing.

The auction companies were viewed with distrust by several of the narrators. There were quite a few accounts of disappointing auction sales. The beautiful 1932 Philadelphia Toboggan carousel from the Palace in Asbury Park, New Jersey, is a case in point. The Palace manager at that time, William Foster, gives the following account of that sale.

> Initially, we weren't going to sell it. We spent a lot of money to restore the carousel and keep it. They put approximately

one hundred thousand dollars into restoration work. The intentions of the owner was to take that carousel and put it in a new location. See, with the redevelopment of the city, everyone knew that the Palace was earmarked to go eventually, within two years, three years, five years. It was really uncertain so we tried to maintain the business as best we could. We put one hundred thousand dollars into the carousel. We put another quarter of a million, let's say, into new machinery, new rides to try and boost our business. We put a lot of money into the Palace to try and maintain it to keep it going.

The Palace really is a landmark in the city and in the shore areas. It's the oldest indoor amusement park. I would say between 1893 and 1895 was when the Palace was built. It's the only indoor park in the state. Well, that summer [1987] we had that ocean pollution problem and business dropped to approximately 55 percent. So we got together and we decided, "Hey, we're knocking our heads against the wall trying to make this business flow and it's not doing it." We never gained back what we had put into it, plus normal costs exceeded our revenue.

We had a girl working for me at the Palace named Susanna Harris. She was doing the restoration work. Her name was fairly well known in the community by this time for doing the work on the carousel. Some people apparently approached her in regards to trying to save the carousel once they found out that it was going to be sold. After spending about two years on restoration, she kinda got attached to it, so she agreed to help out. They formed a committee, Friends of the Carousel, to try to save it. Trying to get donations to try and purchase the carousel whole. But they had no help, really. They were having difficulty to come up with enough money to purchase one horse let alone the entire carousel.

Prior to that sale, the Friends of the Carousel found a benefactor from New York. He was willing to go to a certain amount. The owners wanted more than that. They had the carousel appraised by two different appraisers and they came up with a figure that they felt was what the carousel was going to sell for. They weren't able to match that figure in the negotiations prior to the sale. So they continued on with the sale. I didn't go to the sale, but from what I can determine, there was such a lot of publicity on the carousel in price tag, that once they went to the auction, there was really nobody prepared to purchase it at that price. Everyone was feeling, "Well, I'm not going to get a good deal. It's going to be a certain amount of money so I'm not even going to prepare myself to purchase it." So when they went up there, they found there was not enough interest. The bidding didn't go up high enough.

At the auction, after the carousel wasn't bidding up to expectations, the owner approached the Friends of the Carousel and asked, "are you still willing to purchase it?" 'cause his intentions all the time were to keep it intact and not to sell it in parcel. He was willing to take a loss even to just keep it together. They agreed on a price apparently, so they stopped the auction. Well, the benefactor that was going to give them the money, dropped off with his backing. So, they wound up again not having the money to purchase it. It was a couple days later by the time everyone found out that this guy reneged on his offer. So now, no auction, no sale and we're still holding the carousel and it cost the client about eighty thousand dollars in auctioneer fees. Again lost revenue. So, we wound up going to another auctioneer, Guernsey, and they sold that thing. There was nothing we could do to keep it together. We tried to do the best we could, but it's a business too, and you can't just say, "Well, I'm going to throw a half a million dollars out the window so I can preserve the carousel."

More reports like this and carousel owners may begin to heed National Carousel Association Conservation Chairman Charles Walker's advice to "Hang on to your merry-go-rounds." Charles feels that most amusement parks will be better off in the long run if they keep their old carousel running rather than sending it to the auction block.

7

A Magical Transformation

Whether the carousel was thought of as a work of art or just another amusement device, to keep the merry-go-round looking good, it needed periodic refurbishing. Broken ears, tails, and legs needed to be recarved and replaced. Stripping, sanding, painting, gluing, as well as major structural repairs kept carousel and amusement park owners busy throughout the winter. In the small privately owned amusement park, this often was a family affair. At Eldridge Park, Elmira, New York, Scott Bittler, his brother, and grandfather spent winters renovating the merry-go-round.

> The lion and tiger, my brother and I restored. We spent an entire winter restoring just two figures from the ground up. We were extremely proud of those. It was the primary out of school occupation that my brother and I had during our teens, working in the shop. We would go down after school and on weekends and work in a heated shop area with our grandfather. Often just the three of us there working, sometimes with a couple of other workers. It was a lot of hard work, no doubt about it, but it's something we took a lot of pride in. The summers and the enjoyment of the people on the ride was the payoff. We didn't get rich doing it by any means.

> One of the techniques that the Long family used that I have not observed a whole lot on other merry-go-rounds that I've seen, is a metallic finish on some of the paint color trappings

used on the horses. This metallic look to some of the colors on the trappings was achieved by a technique that my grandfather would hold kind of private as I remember growing up. He would be asked from time to time how this was done and he would refrain from telling them. It was kind of a technique that was passed down within the Long family. It was achieved — I'll give the secret away, and I've done this a number of times myself — by first painting a layer of silver paint on the area and then after that dries, painting the color. These paints — gosh, you can't buy them today — but this particular color paint would be painted over the silver and very quickly wiped off with cloth, leaving the silver showing through the color and giving it a metallic looking appearance. It gives a kind of different dimension to the coloration that you don't find on a lot of animals. So, that's a technique in painting that, as far as I've been able to observe, is somewhat unique to our family.

Another couple of things about the painting that are somewhat unique and traditional to the Long family are some of their color combinations. I don't think you'll find similar color combinations in traditional park paint anywhere. On horses that were black and white body colors, the common trappings that the Long family would use with that were red and green with gold striping. If the horse were brown body color or brown and white, then the trappings that would be used with that are yellow and green with red striping. If the horse body color was gray or gray and white, then red and blue with gold striping would be used on the trappings, or orange and blue with yellow and green striping. For white horses, typically pastel colors would be used for the trappings. And again, either pink and green or pink and blue with gold striping.

And there was one final combination, the palomino color horse would also have typically pastel trappings, sometimes some green and blue with gold striping as well. These were kind of passed down through my grandfather. I don't know that every branch of the Long family would practice this exclusively, but certainly my grandfather did and we did in working with him at Eldridge Park in the restorations that we did there.

One of the things that was very unique about the Eldridge Park machine was that it was not of an original manufacturer's vintage. It was not a whole PTC or a whole Dentzel or a whole Looff machine as most are that you find. It was a menagerie. It was a collection of a number of carvers represented, largely horses. There were fifty-six animals on the ride, two chariots, and only three of the fifty-six animals were other than horses. There was one goat, one lion, and one tiger. The carvers represented included Looff, Dentzel, Carmel — all the outer horses were Carmel. Some of the finest Carmel examples you'll find anywhere, as I've been told and agree with. And also Long.

For the most part the Long representations were in the form of the aluminum replacements that we had sometimes when animals were in restoration. My grandfather Long carved his own horse from scratch that these aluminum ones were made from.

My brother Greg, a Bittler a year or so younger than myself, has bought a small carousel mechanism and has restored the mechanism and is planning on putting together a small carousel comprised of aluminum horses that are reproductions of the wooden horse that my grandfather Long carved, and had an aluminum casting pattern made from it. There are a number of these aluminum horses in raw form that are in storage up in New York state awaiting finishing by my brother for this ride.

One of those aluminum copies I have in the garage, which I've stripped down to bare metal, and am planning on, perhaps, having replicated in fiberglass for the purpose of putting on a rocking stand for kids. Instead of one of these cheap, almost paper mâché looking kinds of rocking horses, to have a real craftsman quality piece. When I grew up myself, one of the first aluminum horses made was on a stand that I grew up rocking on. I grew up with a real rocker, and there really aren't such things out on the market today. It's a smaller horse. It was an inside row size animal, jumper.

The origin of the merry-go-round was primarily from two merry-go-rounds that my grandfather had in his possession at one time. Both of them he acquired from a state of storage in great disrepair. One was a Looff merry-go-round that originally was on the Young's Million Dollar Pier at Atlantic City. So, it comes from a pretty great beginning if you will. He was pretty proud of the fact that he was able to save that machine out of storage from Lord knows where.

One of the things that he did — originally the machine was all standers — and he wanted a jumping horse machine. So, what he did was use the mechanism from the one machine that had jumpers, a jumping mechanism, and make a number of his own modifications to make that all work. Then, he didn't have the jumping horses so he literally converted the stander horses to jumper horses by recarving legs from scratch as jumper legs. The outside row was left to be standers primarily because, well probably because they were all Carmels and he didn't want to touch that original form, but also it's more practical to have standers on the outside of a merry-go-round that's used with a ring machine. It's easier to go for the ring if you've got a stationary horse.

Of course, my grandfather, did a number of restorative kinds of carvings, legs, tails — a number of tails — 'cause all the horses on our ride were originally, or most of them, were horse tails, so he would carve the wooden tail replacements for many of them. And, of course, ears and noses and things that would get broken off. He taught that trade to myself and my brother. That's something I very much enjoyed and would like to do more of. We still have all the carving tools that my grandfather used and we're quite proud of those.

Another piece of evidence to my grandfather's carving talent is exhibited by this framed newspaper article that shows my grandfather sitting atop or on the neck of a dragon head that was mounted to the front of this boat. The boat was a ride on the lake at Eldridge Park. This was, again, an entire original carving of my grandfather's and it adorned this boat for many years before my time. After it came off of the boat, the head itself became — interestingly enough, it was painted in fluorescent paint — and it was mounted to a moving mechanism and put in the spook house. It would jump out under lights that would come on at the last minute. It would jump out at a car coming by it in the spook house. It was a good scary feature in the spook house for a number of years.

At Dreamland Park in Rochester, New York, George Long, Jr., also was doing his own carving and repairs.

My first experience with carving was in 1916. After seeing the Philadelphia Toboggan machine operate, I decided to

Figure 55. George W. Long carving minature horses. Several magazines featured articles on Mr. Long and his carving as did Charles Kuralt, in his "On the Road" series for CBS. (Photo: Courtesy Merrick Price)

make jumpers out of part of the horses on the carousel. In the old days, they were all stationary horses. They all had the legs straight down so on the two inside rows, I cut the legs off and put on jumper legs — a haunched up leg — so I carved those legs. That was my first experience in carving. In 1916, I also had done some work for the Philadelphia Toboggan Company in making rims for other machines, so that I got some experience from them at that time. As a matter of fact while I was with them, I took charge of their building a coaster and a merry-go-round at Shell Pot Park in 1916. America was getting into the war, and they thought that Shell Pot Park would be a good spot for a park during the war period. In Wilmington, Delaware. That's about forty miles south of Philadelphia.

I painted the merry-go-round horses year after year. I don't mean the same horse every year, but between the two machines, the old machine and the new machine, I was kept pretty busy in the wintertime getting them in shape again. You'd have broken legs, broken ears, that sort of thing. I had to build the legs sturdier too because the kids all used to

125

hang around the outsides, you know, and grab rings and that was hard on the horses. They'd pull a ring out, and the ring would hit the horse's neck probably and put a dent in it. You had all those things to bother with.

The horses on this carousel that we bought — the new one in 1915 — were soft poplar. Before that, the horses were made of bass wood. Now it must be that the Philadelphia Toboggan Company had a chance to buy a carload of poplar and the legs were too weak. The slender part of the leg would break right here. I had more trouble with broken legs on that new machine than I ever had on the old machine.

The kids can't pull the tails out now because the new machine that we bought from the Philadelphia Toboggan Company had wooden tails. The old machine had real tails. There weren't enough tails to go around anymore because they were building lots of merry-go-rounds and there were less and less horses on the road when the automobile came in. They couldn't find enough tails so they started to make wooden ones.

Figure 56. This horse on PTC #36 at Dreamland-Seabreeze, Rochester, New York, was known as "the Indian" before restoration. "It has an Indian up here, with a bow across the front" — Susan Hofsass. PTC #36 was destroyed by fire in 1994. (Photo: Courtesy George W. Long)

126

Anyone thinking of restoring an entire merry-go-round might get some idea of the amount of work involved from Dr. Floyd Moreland's description of the renovation of the carousel at Seaside Heights, New Jersey. Dr. Moreland had loved the merry-go-round from childhood and had worked on it as a teenager and summers during his college years. When he learned that the carousel was to be sold, he wrote to the then owner, Kenneth Wynne.

I asked him if indeed it was for sale. It had been many years since we had contact. He wrote back. It was a very warm cordial letter about the family and such, and then he did say yes, it was for sale. Then a few months went by and I kept pondering, and it was breaking my heart to think that this was going to go 'cause I, as a child, always thought that it was constant.

There was a buyer, out of Washington state, but for some reason, the sale fell through. Then, I decided, "Well look, maybe I can just have a swan song, maybe it's not so stupid to think of a professor running a merry-go-round." So, I wrote Ken again one night, and I said, "This is a very serious question and don't laugh, but would you allow a college professor to run the merry-go-round on weekends for awhile?" I wanted to say goodbye to it. He responded with a phone call and said "the answer is yes, and you start such and such a date." So back I came to run the carousel.

I was thrilled to run it again. But as I did, I was sad as I knew that eventually it would go. I ran it all that summer during the weekends. I was looking at it and thought it's so shabby looking. Mechanically, it was perfect, but it had been allowed just to sit because the intent was to sell, so why paint it? So, one day near the end of the summer, I said to Ken, "You know, this should really be that color, and that should be fixed, and the fluorescent lights — there used to be fluorescent lights on this. It was horrible — they should come out and incandescent bulbs should be put back in." He said, "Well, you know, it's really not in our budget." I said, "Well, could I redo the carousel in the winter?" He said, "Well, let me ponder it." Within a week, I got a note from him saying, "You have carte blanche to do whatever you want to with your carousel."

Then I got a key to the building and that was magic. The afternoon I got the key to the building, I think I came back here four or five times that night to be sure it worked. I couldn't believe I had a key to the building. Then we — we meaning a very close friend of mine, Elaine Egues, who is an administrator at City University — she and I and my mother and step father were the principle workers. A few other people were added on. We chose colors. We went out and bought paint. We erected scaffolds.

What I know about carousels and carousel art, I know from books and observation, visiting carousels. I'm certainly not an artist so we never thought we were restoring. That would involve total stripping, documentation of original colors, going layer by layer. Much more than we had the time, the money or the skill to do. I like to call it a kind of rehabilitation. What we wanted to do was make the carousel sparkle. I wanted so much, in the spring when we opened, for people to walk in here and oooh and aaah. The one thing that kept sort of depressing me all winter as we worked so hard was fear that no one would notice. I kept telling Elaine, "I don't know that anybody's even going to notice." This was my dream. I was, by the way, redoing it as I remembered it as a child. I chose the colors from memory. I'm sure, if I could go back in a time machine, it's not quite the same. But in my memory, it's very close now to what I envisioned.

The director of operations for the whole amusement pier, and a lot of other workers, mechanics and electricians, were very fond of this carousel. This carousel generates a lot of affection here, and, I think everyone was saddened that it was going to be removed. When we started working on it, they all offered assistance. The vertical lights were all fluorescent before, so someone built the cases for me and did the wiring. At no cost. I mean they just did it. And a variety of other things were done by the staff. There were broken legs on some of the animals. One of the carpenters who works downstairs carved out some new legs — he's very gifted — and doweled them in. So everyone became involved in some way in this what I think is a magical transformation.

The outside, the rim, which is called a rounding board, is in eighteen sections. Now when you look at the outside, you'll see that they are intricate carvings. After I did the first section, which took me forever, I thought, "Oh, my God, I'm

Figure 57. "The outside, the rim, which is called a rounding board, is in eighteen sections. Now when you look at the outside, you'll see that they are intricte carvings. After I did the first section, which took me forever, I thought, 'Oh, my God, I'm never going to get around this'" — Floyd L. Moreland. (Photo: Dr. Norma B. Menghetti)

never going to get around this." Then, just to protect myself, I worked with every other one thinking that at least if I do every other one, every other one will look beautiful and every other one will look shabby, and maybe I can get by. There was a point when we thought we would never finish, that it was just too much. And we were balancing this with our jobs so it was an incredible job.

We pushed so hard because it was getting colder and colder. The only kind of heater that I could get in here were these butane heaters. They blow and the flames come out the back. I don't know the technical name, but those scare me because I'm very afraid of fire in here. So, I would only use it occasionally to warm my fingers so that they'd move again. Quite seriously. But pretty much by about mid January we couldn't do anything else so we had to stop. And then as soon as it got a little bit warm — and by a little bit warm, I mean thirty-five degrees. That was warm. Back we came to put on the finishing touches.

We opened the carousel in mid March that year on a very warm day. Elaine puts it best. Elaine was in the theater many years ago, and she said it was like opening night. The people did oooh and aaah. As I say that, I get goose bumps because I remember that day so vividly. People just came in and looked. Several people walked down the board walk and walked in and said to me, "Has this carousel been here for long?" And I said, "Well, it's been here since 1937." "We've been coming here for X years. We never knew it was here." What had happened, it was so bright and beautiful that people noticed. And it's been all going upwards since then, I'm pleased to say. Each winter, we do a little more work. We pull something else down. It's an on-going process. It never ends.

Originally, if you look up high, those paintings there. Those are oils and there are eighteen of them. All but two are original with the carousel. Two are replacements. But originally, there were paintings where this mirror is and all here. All

Figure 58. Santa Clause rides in the chariot on the historic Floyd L. Moreland Carousel in Seaside Heights, New Jersey. This is one of the few carousels in the United States, possibly the only one, to be operated on Christmas Day, and Christmas Eve, and New Years Day, Easter, Memorial Day, the 4th of July, Thanksgiving, and all holidays that fall on weekends, all year long. (Photo: Dr. Norma B. Menghetti)

oil paintings. I hate these mirrors by the way. One day they're going. What happened was in the early fifties, someone pulled all those paintings out and put in cartoon faces. It was Donald Duck and Mickey Mouse all here and all in here. I wanted it to go back to its antique look. We couldn't find the paintings, and I believe they were thrown out. The mirrors were a stop gap. It's temporary. Someday a lot of this will be changed. I would love to get an artist to do paintings here.

If repainting carousel horses is left to the younger members of the family, one may not be quite satisfied with the finished product. And sometimes, even the mature owners would make mistakes. Justin Van Vliet discloses how he and his grandfather took the easy way in painting their Allan Herschell merry-go-round.

At my grandfather's house in Garfield, we used to store the horses in the basement. Had racks built for them. Set them right on. And, we'd start in this corner and work our way around. Take the horses out. Fix it. We had a man by the name of Edgar Steppe. He was a frustrated carpenter. He used to carve the new legs and everything to look just like the old one. He'd build new legs for them. We'd bolt them on and drill a hole, put pegs in it and whatnot. It was a job. We used to work about two and a half hours a night down in the basement painting the horses and whatnot. Sometimes on a Saturday, especially if the weather was bad outside, my grandfather and I worked down there all day during the winter months. That's what we used to do most every night, repair the horses and paint them. All our horses had jewels along the saddle blanket. I know one year we painted them and we covered over them. My grandmother raised a stink. She said we covered up all the good parts of the horse. We had to clean them all off. She insisted that we clean them.

We had this one horse with an American flag draped on it. My grandfather, he liked the Lone Ranger. So, one year, he got the bright idea to paint the horse silver and match it with the American flag. So, the first opening night of the season, which was in Garfield Park, we had to take the horse off the machine 'cause all the kids wanted to ride the Lone Ranger's horse. We had to take the horse off the machine 'cause they were tearing the horse apart. Boy, I mean, we never did that again. The following morning, my grandfather was out there repainting the horse. He painted it white. He had trouble with the white, so he finally wound up painting it gray.

Once the Martha's Vineyard Preservation Trust purchased the Flying Horses carousel, former Executive Director, Jane Chittick recounts that the next step was to restore it.

The first thing we've done with the proceeds is to plow it back into the horses themselves. We had a major restoration done by Rosa Ragan of Raleigh, North Carolina a year ago. I flew down to Raleigh during the restoration. The horses were all shipped down there and returned. It's sort of in their un-painted state and lined up side by side that you could actu-ally distinguish different sculptors or carvers. There would be perhaps a group of three or four horses that clearly were done by the same person, the next few by someone else. There's one that really stood out as being sort of the ugly duckling of the crew. Clearly an apprentice had started on that horse. He was not very talented. Things were just terri-bly distorted. Eyes were sort of lopsided, different levels and ears were backwards. And then, this sort of awful leer. He looked rather evil. I mentioned that to Rosa Ragan and she said she had noticed the same thing. Her husband had called him the "Devil Horse" because he did look sort of like this flaring, evil spirit. And other people would come in and say, "Oh, that horse looks strange." So, by the end of it, Rosa began to feel sorry for him and when he was painted, she painted one of the teeth gold. That was to make him feel better and to make him feel special because he was differ-ent. So, all of the school children who know the story now want to see the *Devil Horse*, and they look for the gold tooth. Some people feel, I think, more protective of him. I think he will be the one, of all the ones, best remembered.

The second phase is the restoration, the conservation of the original oil paintings. We don't have them all, but we have about three quarters of them. Those are being restored by Westlake Conservators in Skaneateles, New York. They are wonderful scenes of ocean going vessels, lots of river scenes of paddle boats, people in outdoor recreation, riding

Figure 59. "All of the school children who know the story now want to see the *Devil Horse,* and they look for the gold tooth" — Jane Chittick. (Photo: Alison Shaw)

> bicycles, on horses. Lovely scenes of the countryside. Very bucolic and pastoral. Lake and mountains. Really reminiscent of the Hudson River School.

As interest in merry-go-rounds and carousel figures as works of art developed quickly, new carousel related businesses came into existence with comparable rapidity. In particular, restorers and restoration firms developed because they met a growing need for authentic repair and renovation. Neither merry-go-round owners nor carousel enthusiasts were content to have their newly acquired *objet d'art* preserved with park paint. Renovations had to be thorough and done by a professional. Restor-

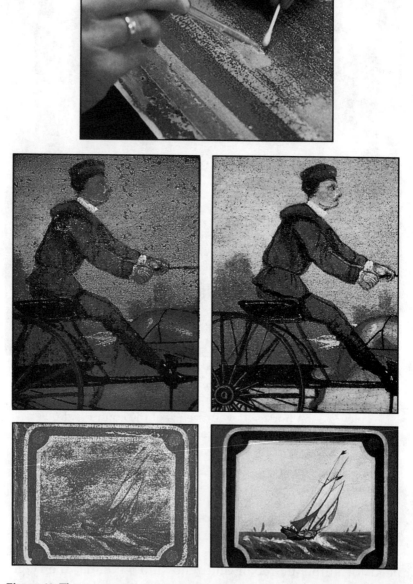

Figure 60. The conservation of the Flying Horses carousel of Martha's Vinyard was done by Westlake Conservators. **Top:** Initial cleaning. **Middle:** Detail of racing cart before (left) and after (right) treatment. **Bottom:** Sailing boat scene before (left) and after (right) treatment. (Photo: Westlake Conservators)

ers and conservators sprang up everywhere to meet the growing demand. Some were excellent and others were careless to the extent of actually damaging the articles they repaired.

One of the better known firms noted for excellent restoration work is R & F Designs in Bristol, Connecticut. The shop started out in a garage, and, in less than four years, had gross revenues of more than a million dollars. The heart of this success was the quality work done by R & F Designs owner Bill Finkenstein and his team of experts.

I had done those first three horses. I liked them but there was something. You know, as an artist you never get better if you say, "I'm good." You always strive to do something better. I looked at these pieces that I had just worked on and I used artistic license. I kind of did what I felt. I got excited and I painted them, but there was more there.

When you walk around those horses, there's magic. It's something special. I wanted to say that not only did they look beautiful in their day, and they do today, but there's history behind them. There's the story of the immigrants that came to this country with these fantastic skills and shared them with all of us. And the beauty. And the talent that was there. They came with their little satchel of tools and that was their start in America. Really, though carousels were European before they were even American, the art form didn't take off and come alive till it came to this country. I've got my own feeling about that. This has got nothing to do with history, but my own feeling. If you take a look at European carousels, they're very boxy. They're very straight forward. They've got some fanciful things on 'em, but for the most part they were very straight looking. But here, these carvers came to America and I've got to believe they felt every bit of the freedom that was afforded them as artists, and all of a sudden, their [the horses] heads went up and the tongues came out and the legs kicked up. It was there. You can see it, and that's what makes our carousels here in this country so much more beautiful and flamboyant.

So, I wasn't so sure that I was doing the right thing at that point. That's when it dawned on me. I had just taken courses in genealogy, and found out that you should make sure you talk to all the older people in your family because once they're gone, those stories are gone. So, I used that same logic

135

in this business. I got on the phone and I called everybody that I could find a listing about that's involved in this business. People like Fred Fried, Charlotte Dinger, Barney Illions, the lady in New Mexico, Marianne Stephens.

Well, as a result of that, I struck up a great friendship with Barney Illions. It did not last very long. He died. But, before he passed away, he sent me a little booklet and it says *Marcus Charles Illions & Sons, Methods of Shop Operations*. It was like he gave me the Family Bible. And It was so exciting to say, "Yes, this is the way you approach something like this," because I'm not so worried about Bill Finkenstein the artist being remembered here. I would rather have a piece of history saved, something that we can share.

It's kind of humorous to think of how we started. We started from a garage. It wasn't very big and we were running out of room. So, we looked around and we found a rent, a turn-of-the-century funeral parlor. Couldn't get a lot of people to work at night [laughter]. But, it was a fun place. Just the age of the building and everything else added to what we were doing, but we still didn't have enough room. And we kept growing. I mean, I had a horse by the reins and I couldn't slow him down.

This business is unique in the sense that we have done very little advertising. People have come to us and said, "Gee, this is an interesting story." Or, they'll come to us and say, "We heard about you through such and such and we have a carousel." It's really been word of mouth and that has been exciting. It's to the honor of all that work under this roof, because there's some very talented people here.

Here we were. We went to the turn-of-the-century funeral parlor. We kept growing. I said, "I've got to find some place. With what I'm paying for rent and everything else, it would be easier if I could find someplace that I could call my own." So, we rode down the street one day, and looked up and here was this building. It was in tough shape. It was a turn-of-the-century factory that had kind of been left alone all of these years. We came in. We put in two-hundred-eighty windows. We sand blasted all the old wood so that you could see the beautiful beams that are in this building. My brother-in-law had just gotten his contractor's license for electrical so he re-wired everything. My uncles came in and did that beautiful carpeting you saw downstairs. It was really a fam-

Figure 61. Carousel restorer and artist Bill Finkenstein demonstrates painting techniques on a griffin at a fair in Connecticut. (Photo: Courtesy Bill Finkenstein)

ily and friend oriented endeavor. What I look back now and laugh at, we all remember the story of the Emperor with no clothes. I would bring people in here early on and walk them around and it was a mess. Nobody said, "Bill, you're naked." "It doesn't look like what you're telling me" [laughter]. It has happened. I mean, the years have gone by and it keeps growing.

Lake Compounce in Bristol, Connecticut, was the first [complete] carousel that we restored. As a result of that one, Lighthouse Point, New Haven saw what we were doing. They came down. Then Bridgeport came down. Then Crescent Park, East Providence, Rhode Island. I can almost remember in succession all the different ones that came to us.

Shortly after I was working on the one from East Providence, a couple of men knocked at my door and this big man with a southern drawl said, "Hello, ah'm Bo Bassage," and he says, "We've come here to take a look at your operation." They came in. They took a look at what we did and they said, "Yes, we want you to do our carousel." That very day [we got the New Orleans City Park carousel].

Figure 62. The lion from the City Park carousel in New Orleans, Louisiana, undergoes a chemical bath to remove layers of park paint. This system of allowing chemicals to flow over the specimen preserves the wood better than dip stripping or heat guns. (Photos: Beau Bassich)

Figure 63. The restored lion, with his vibrant color, brilliant eyes, and ferocious jaw, takes his place back on the Carmel/Looff carousel at City Park in New Orleans, Louisiana. (Photo: Beth McFarland)

We went down to take it apart and bring 'em up. When they do something in New Orleans, they do it big. They had a party when they sent the horses out and they had a party when they brought 'em back. We have tapes of all that. Hopefully, in the future, we're going to do something very special and bring a tape out of that whole restoration from beginning to end. There were three, I think, awards [National Trust for Historic Preservation] given in regards to that particular carousel. One to the park. One to us and one to another firm that worked on that project with Bo. It was a great honor.

Again, sometimes you wonder as you start into business and you start doing certain things, if indeed you're doing the right thing. Wouldn't it have been easier to spray paint the horses? Wouldn't it have been easier to use the epoxies? Wouldn't it have been easier and cost us less money to do a lot of different things? Then, all of a sudden, somebody recognizes the effort that you've put in and how much it really means to you. They recognized that and they gave us that

Figure 64. Top: A 1906 photo of the City Park carousel pavilion. The building, which is twelve sided with a three-tiered roof and stained glass windows, was built around the turn-of-the-century. (Photo: Courtesy Louisiana Collection, Tulane University). **Bottom:** In 1965, the City Park carousel pavilion's stained glass clerestory windows and cupola were still intact, but in need of repair. (Photo: Leon Trice, Sr.)

award. And that's special because it's an award for every-body under this roof. That's just a real nice honor and it will spur us on to, hopefully, do even better things as time goes on.

I have people that come in to me all the time and they say, "Bill, why don't you use polyurethanes? Give you better, harder finish. Clear. Quick. They won't yellow. Why don't you use epoxies? They'll give you stronger bonding. Why don't you use more fillers? You know the plastic fillers are real good for the cracks. Use those. Why don't you use acrylics? You'll be able to paint the horses faster. Use your spray gun more." All of these things. I'll tell you why I don't do that. Because it wasn't done originally. Number one. These animals are around here today because the old timers must have known what they were doing. There was a special pride in it. I wanted to stay as true as I could to time.

Hopefully, we've been innovative in the sense of our thought of going back to what made it happen to begin with. The old hide glues in the crock pot. We heat up the glue. We take all that time to do that. Why? Not because it isn't faster to go to epoxy, but because that's what they used. There's a rule of thumb in the art restoration field and that is never do anything to a piece of art that you can't reverse. A lot of these epoxies, you can't reverse the epoxies. You can't re-verse the polyurethanes. So, if you start working with these things, you don't know what trouble you're going to make later on.

Each horse, each animal that comes in here, each item has its unique problems. That's the first thing we do, is to assess those problems. We tape, we photograph before we even start. Then we look and see how we're going to handle this. It's kinda like Pandora's box. Until you take all of those lay-ers of paint off, what might not look too bad on the surface, can look like heck underneath.

There was a couple of things that we found over the years. It wasn't just that it was happening at one park. It kinda happened universally. They must have called around and said, "Hey, this is the way to do it." Did you ever see the corrugated fasteners on the back of an old frame? They're kind of little wavy metal nailed in to pull everything tight together. Well somebody came up with the brilliant idea way back then that, as the seams opened up a little bit, nail those things in there and that will keep everything nice and tight. The problem is that condensation builds up around the metal and you get wood rot.

Other things happened even closer to now and this is sad. If anybody remembers the Danbury Fair, the Danbury Carousel. There's a mall up there now. There's a carousel in that mall. Lot of people think that's the original one. It isn't. The original one something terrible happened. It happened out of ignorance of not knowing what to do to save their pieces. They took their animals and they wrapped them in fiberglass, thinking that, "Well, if you put fiberglass around, it will protect the beautiful carvings underneath," and someday, they'd be able to restore them. Well, what happened is condensation built up between the wood and the fiberglass, and they became cocoons. They all just fell apart inside. So, everyone of those animals, for the most part, were lost. At least their legs were lost and most of the trappings because it starts to rot from the surface down. Just crumbles up. So, they lost the whole carousel. These were things that happened.

There isn't a week that goes by that somebody doesn't at least call you about something or bring something in to take a look at it. All the time. Gee, what's next? We're finding these things out. We continue to learn. As I said earlier, when you say you're the best or you're good, you don't get any better. That's not what we have here. I say we because this place here is still the many, many talented people we've got. As they come in and they go to work for us, we tell them, "The man that picks up the sand paper and goes back and forth is as important as the man that puts on the pin stripe out in the other room with the gold leaf." They're all so important to what we have. If you sand too much, you can take detail off. You can lose a piece of history instead of saving it. If you don't paint authentically and take the time to lay it in that groove nice, it can look terrible. So, we're all intertwined here, and there's a lot of pride.

Toni Grekin, Cultural Affairs Director for the City of Binghamton, New York, verifies both that past mistakes had been made in restoration of the Broome County carousels and that R & F Designs deserves its fine reputation.

I don't think George F. Johnson or the Allan Herschell Company when they built these carousels expected them to be operating in sixty years. What was done was done out of ignorance more than out of neglect. Obviously paint jobs had to keep happening. Well, they didn't have them done by artists. They had them done by the public works guys. In fact, I was told of this story where somebody, who is now the Parks Department Director for the City of Binghamton, that his predecessor by two administrations or something had been involved. They just kind of had a party and painted the horses and signed their names on them. It was just done by the public works guys. "What color do you want, Murray? How about chartreuse?" And that's really how they were painted. In fact, keeping them painted protected the wood.

However, there wasn't a real lot of knowledge about how one goes about this [restoration]. The first thing that we did, I believe the whole herd from Rec Park was taken to a strip-

Figure 65. An aerial view of the carousel building which is located in the C. Fred Johnson Park at Johnson City, New York, circa 1950. The swimming pool in the foreground of the picture is no longer there. The carousel building is eighteen-sided with a six-sided cupola. (Photo: Ed Aswad, Carriage House Photography)

per in Portland, and they were bath stripped to get off the old paint. That was not such a good idea. What that did was then undermine whatever the original gluing had been and the colors. Shortly after, seams started showing up and being exposed. What should have happened at that time, we should have gone in very quickly to have closed those up and repainted those, and that wasn't done.

The city sent me to the National Carousel Association annual convention in 1989. We felt we needed more information. That we couldn't approach this blindly as we had done the last restoration. I wanted to hear from those most knowledgeable, "Who do you think are the best restorers in the country?" "What are the issues?" "Where are my concerns?" "What are the questions I should be asking?" And I got the most wonderful, wonderful advice. When I came back, they sent me these wonderful magazines that keep us abreast. They sent me two huge volumes of manuals with carousel operating [information]. And they will send them to anybody who is a carousel operator. You didn't even have to be

Figure 66. The carousel building in Ross Park, Binghamton, New York. Its 1920 carousel is the oldest of the six Broome County carousels. (Photo: Ed Aswad, Carriage House Photography)

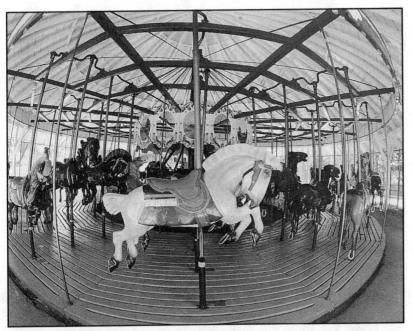

Figure 67. The Ross Park carousel was restored in 1989. It is a spectacular four-abreast carousel with sixty different horses, a gorilla chariot and a maiden's chariot. (Photo: Ed Aswad, Carriage House Photography)

a member for this. That really gave us the nuts and bolts to start the process with. It covered everything from fund-raising to the gears themselves, to the horses, to the floor, everything. Everything you might need to know.

Out of that convention, I kept getting the names of five people who were considered better than anyone else in the country. The same five names kept cropping up. Bill Finkenstein was one of those people. Also, he had just won the National Trust for Historic Preservation award. They had given Bill an award the year before for doing the last carousel in Louisiana, down in New Orleans. That was, of course, very impressive to us.

All of our horses, except for two that are going to the County Historical Society, are in Connecticut right now [1990]. I would say a third of them have been completely restored. He started on the project in March. Bill is quite marvelous.

Pride in doing your best work was a common theme with all those involved with carousel restoration. Kenneth Lynch, who has restored many of the pieces in the Charlotte Dinger collection, recalls his first meeting with her.

I had finished carving my son's rocking horse, which looked more like a carousel horse than not. The carver's club had a show and tell type table, and I happened to bring it down. It was a night when this older fellow happened to be there. And he was so impressed by my work that he told me he knows of a woman who collects all the pieces, and it turned out to be Charlotte Dinger. He introduced me to her, and I brought up the piece that I had made for my son, my carousel rocking horse. She was impressed enough to ask me if I was interested in doing any restoration work for her. And I've been doing that ever since. It's gone on just about seven years that I've been working with her.

I do it as a hobby, part-time if you will. She is such an avid collector that she has so many pieces that she has enough work for me to do probably for the next ten years if I wanted or more. I have three pieces that we're working on. Three horses. One happens to be a Looff jumper, which someone else had restored some years ago, and really did a lousy job. The piece should have been completely taken apart and re-constructed, 'cause a lot of the glue joints have separated, and they put it back together using screws and nails and whatever, and that's not the typical restoration job that she looks to have done.

I do everything but the final painting. In other words, I take the horse that's maybe in a stripped condition, disassemble things that have to be reassembled correctly. If pieces are missing, I'll recarve those, reapply those, and get the whole job back to a sealer prime type coat for the final paint job.

I don't know if you go into Zodiac signs or anything like that, but I'm born in May and a Taurus is more like an earthy type person, somewhat artistic I guess, but good with their hands. They take a lot of pride in what they do, according to the people that write the horoscopes. For me to do a certain thing — people always say I'm a perfectionist — however, I never really view it that way. I just look at it to do the best job that I can do, each and every time. Evidently, as far as

Charlotte Dinger was concerned, she felt that I would always take it a couple steps past anybody else. Because it's a part of me going back into it too, and she seemed to appreciate it.

8

Friends of Our Carousels

Promoting a carousel or marketing an amusement park in the old days was often a full time business in itself. No one did it better than Sol Abrams, publicist for Palisades Amusement Park in Cliffside, New Jersey, for more than thirty years. Seven days a week, Sol worked on creating stories that would get in the newspapers and newsreels, stories that would bring not only the press but also the people to Palisades. Sol's promotional strategies were so successful that the small park just across the Hudson River from New York City became one of the best known and most loved amusement parks in the United States. Many of Sol's creative stunts might serve as examples for contemporary parks or for "Friends of Our Carousels" working to promote and preserve merry-go-rounds today.

The first assignment, I recall very vividly. Opening day. We always did some really zany news making pre-opening event. Like, we would have the world's biggest spring cleaning event. There was more soap and water used in the Spring clean up, to clean up the midway and the rides, than there would be in all the kitchens in a city of ten thousand. We used figures. We used to do the story about all the bulbs being replaced. A million light bulbs and six miles of neon tubing. And paint. We'd show the painters painting. We had fifty-five different shades of pastel colors. What Palisades Amusement Park did was paint every inch differently every year. Most people wouldn't paint their homes every two,

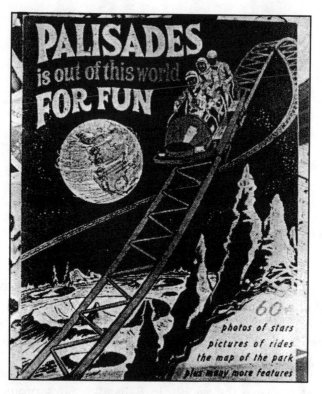

Figure 68. In 1969, for its seventy-second year of continuous operation, Palisades Amusement Park issued a souvenir booklet that told about the various rides, attractions and contests. In addition to selling for sixty cents, it also was filled with advertisements that brought in additional revenues. (Photo: Courtesy Richard W. Glasheen)

three, or four years. We used to paint the park, every midway, and every ride, we would paint. Fresh paint. In addition to that, we would bring in new rides, and we would change the locations of the rides, so that to people coming in, the park would have a totally new look. The Spring cleaning was the first kick off.

We all take television for granted, but television just started, like in 1948, ABC for example. Very few people could afford television sets in those days. We made a deal, if you want to call it that, with a company that was manufacturing Pilot television sets. We would have drawings every Wednesday night to win television sets. The portables or the table top models weighed a ton. They weighed as much as a refrigerator. We would have people winning those sets. Not everybody had automobiles in those days. They had no way of taking them home. People would have to take taxi cabs to New York. I would phone in the local angle stories to the papers. That was big news in those days — a little story about somebody winning a television set.

The crowds were very good. And this was without going into the fancy terms they use in marketing and in doing market research today. All we were interested in was getting people into the park, the principle of bringing people in. We already had the Diaper Derby, the world champion baby crawling race. The Mrs. America contest originated at Palisades. Then, I started the Miss American teenager Pageant, Little Miss America, Miss American Starlet, and Miss Polish America, with a polka party every week. These people would never in the world come to an amusement park, but I got older people because their children were in it. Ethnic pride. And Miss Latin America. I did ethnic promotions when nobody wanted to touch the Hispanics.

The Little Miss America pageant was the biggest traffic builder in the park. I would have two thousand kids show up three days a week all summer long. And they went zoom, zoom off through the stage like army battalions. But each one of those kids brought their aunts, their uncles, their mothers, their fathers, the brothers, and they spent money in the park. Everything was a beauty pageant. We had more Queens, Misses and Sweethearts there than they had in all the history books. But it drew in traffic.

I franchised the Miss America Teenager Pageant. I had it franchised to fifty parks in the country. Each park paid a fee, and a park in Oregon, or Washington, or Dallas, wherever it might be was advertising: THE WINNER GOES TO PALISADES AMUSEMENT PARK. That had other parks advertising and publicizing us across America.

There's a lot of things going on now that the park was so far ahead of. For example, we hired the retirees, the senior citizens. We were the first ones in the amusement park industry to do this and it paid off with many dividends. Many of them were doctors, bankers, and lawyers. They wanted to have a few hours to go out during the day to be with people. The women, we made them cashiers. In the kiddie park, we only had grandparents. We wouldn't dare put a teenager in the kiddie park because if a girl walked by in a mini skirt, a young male ride operator would turn his head away and the kid might fall off the ride. These grandparents took care of every kid on the rides like they were their own grandchildren. So, it worked. They showed up. There were never any complaints. They weren't out drinking at night. And they appreciated it.

In the same way, we were way ahead of the time with safety and security. There was never any problem. We had no racial problems. We had the system and we laid down the law. New York city could use our system today.

We used to do a Triplets Convention. As a publicity stunt, not as an attraction, but it got us publicity all over the world. Now today with the fertility pills, triplets, multiple birth, it's not unusual. But in those days, we would get quadruplets and triplets, one-hundred-fifty sets of triplets. The movies news reels would conduct these events. Do the stories every year. Of concessionaires and ride operators going through mid day nightmares as the kids hit the turnstiles in threes.

Once a week we would get in the newsreels, and they went into the theaters. I would have a Beautiful Legs Contest every year. I would go into Macy's and get the largest pillow cases, cut openings for eyes and arms in them. It was a staged event. We'd have the girls on the runway. We'd set up some bald headed men leering at them. Then, when the winner was selected, we would lift up the sheet, and it probably would be the homeliest girl, but with the most beautiful legs.

Every week we had the aerial act, the acrobats and the aerialists, and we would highlight these people and turn it into a news making event. One year we had an aerialist group that was billed as the Worlds Greatest — everybody was the Worlds Greatest. They were called the Triska Troupe and they had the Worlds Youngest Aerialist. They had an infant that would walk the wire with them on the father's shoulders. This was back in the days of the newsreels. The newsreel people were legendary. They were daredevils. They would fight to get the picture. One day, this Max Markman from Universal Newsreel was shooting this aerialist act. All the other newsreel people would climb up one ladder at one end of the wire to shoot it from one angle. They would get down, climb up the other side and get it from the other angle.

This is before a packed audience of several thousand people. Well, Max Markman, not even thinking to climb down, just walked with his camera over the wire, balancing himself. The audience roared and applauded him, and the act wanted to kill him. The act was supposed to be flirting with death and he killed the act.

We did a lot of charity days too. Every year, we used to run an outing for the New York City Police Anchor Club for fourteen thousand orphans and underprivileged children. We closed the park to the public one day a season. We gave them the park and we also gave them the busses and all the food and the entertainment. The fourteen thousand orphans and underprivileged children were from all races and all religions and all different areas. Chinese, the Catholic homes with nuns. All groups. They came from the Jewish homes and the poor settlement houses. Then we would call up the vendors who sold to us and the ice cream companies. Can you imagine I got fourteen thousand box lunches from Horn and Hardart every year. They donated them. I got Hostess cakes, Seven-Up, Coca-Cola, Pepsi-Cola. All the performers came out to entertain. Those kids had a day. And there were five hundred off-duty uniformed police and nuns that came as escorts with the kids.

The nuns used to go around and have a good time for themselves. They went on the roller coaster and we just caught them with a picture that showed three nuns on the ride. There was a movie out at the time with Sally Fields called *The Flying Nun*. This picture was called *The Flying Coaster*. That picture appeared all over the country and the world.

We were a show room. This Mickey Hughes went into the ride importing business. You cannot have a showroom in New York or anyplace else for a ninety foot carousel. So, what do you do? You have your showroom at the park. He'd lease the rides. He brought them in. We were the first ones to get any of these new rides every year. And we would always advertise, two million dollars in new rides, featuring this ride and that ride.

Everything we did we turned into a promotion. We used every gimmick. On the back of match books we had advertising. We used to work with all of the radio and TV stations. I used to trade time, air time. They would give me fifty thousand dollars or a hundred thousand dollars worth of air time. I would give them fifty thousand dollars or a hundred thousand dollars worth of space in the park or near the park or on drinking cups or match books to publicize their name. I would throw in a contest for them. I had Miss WRCA TV before it was NBC. Or Miss Channel Four. I was doing a lot of remotes from the park. During the summer, we had more television originating from the park than you had at Rockefeller Center. And this exposure, you couldn't buy.

We did so many things. We tried to attract people of all ages. I used to bring these kiddie stars up every week. Popeye, Tom Corbett, Space Cadet. His name was Frankie Corbett, who played in *Boystown* with Mickey Rooney. Paul Trippe from Mr. Imagination. Jack McCarthy, Cliff Robertson. He had a show called Rod Brown of the Rocket Rangers. I had the original Clarabelle, with Bob Keeschan. Bob Keeschan was Captain Kangaroo. He was Corny the Clown before he became Captain Kangaroo. I never paid an act for anything, except the circus. I had all the Kiddie shows. I was a promoter. That's what I was getting paid for. I got all the stars, the Eddie Fishers and Vic Damones, the Tony Bennetts, The Supremes, The Temptations, every recording artist. I got them to come up gratis because I promoted them on the air. In those days I had two million in air time. It would be like fifty million today. I'd do things for every age level to get people in. From the Diaper Derby to the swimming grand-mother.

Coming back to the carousel, when Irving Rosenthal bought the park in 1934, it came with a Dentzel. But Irving sold that carousel, to get the one that he had. And the story was that it came from the 1893 Chicago Exposition. It didn't. For years I was publicizing it that way and everybody believed it. I didn't find out about it until we went to disassemble it, 'cause the center pole said 1928. It was a Philadelphia Toboggan. I can not begin to tell you how many commercials were done on that carousel.

In the amount of rides, Palisades Amusement Park was number one. In acreage, it was probably one of the smallest. Nobody could believe we had only 38 acres. The unique thing was. . . today, it's the site of high rises. In our time, we had "high rises". We put one ride on top of another. We had to make space. It was small, but it was number one in rides and it was number one in publicity. Without a doubt, Palisades was the most publicized park in the world.

We can see variations of Sol's advertising techniques in several of the other interviews, with many of the promotions still being used today. Like Sol running raffles at Palisades to develop public interest in the park, two narrators used raffles to promote their carousels and develop public awareness of the beauty and history of the American merry-go-round. Along with drawings for a prize, Robert Bennett at Seaside Heights, New Jersey, developed a scheme of selling half-price tickets over the Easter weekend.

> What we've done to try to stimulate business for our merry-go-round here, we bought a replica of fiberglass of a full-sized merry-go-round horse. Every person that buys a ticket and goes on to our merry-go-round also gets a free chance on that full-size replica. On Labor Day weekend, we have a drawing and we give that person the replica of our carousel horse. Last year [1989] was our first year. I forget the person's name now. Floyd Moreland has it and we're going to be putting their picture up each year. We'll continue this. We've already started this year.
>
> We do all kinds of local advertising. We have a thing here Easter weekend. We just advertise it in Ocean County. It's kind of a thing for the neighbors, what we call our neighbors, the people that live in the surrounding area. We sell half-price tickets for Waterpark and for the Pier rides. Now, these tickets, they can buy as many as they want and they're good all summer long. Why we do that is because we never

Figure 69. Advertising the Floyd L. Moreland Carousel as "Historic" on the ticket has helped to make the public aware of the significance of the classic Dentzel/Looff carousel. (Courtesy Floyd L. Moreland)

want to hear one of our neighbors say, "Oh, gee, that ride was too much money." Well, if you feel it's too much money, you can come any Easter Sunday you want and pay half-price. This, year, we're doing it Saturday and Sunday. We always had Easter as our opening day, and we used to open Easter Sunday. But now we have started opening Easter Saturday, so now we'll have that special on Easter weekend. They can come and buy as many tickets as they want at half-price and the tickets are good all summer.

What happens is, every year it seems like somebody that's a little skeptical in the beginning, they'll come up and they'll say, "Oh, give me twenty dollars worth of tickets," if they've got grandchildren or children. Then, they find out maybe before July is over, they ran out of tickets. Now, they have to go pay the regular price, they say, "Why didn't I buy more?" So, now when they come back the next year, they buy more. We have a lot of motels even buying them in town.

And Pepsi-Cola comes out with a two liter bottle. They put a coupon on that bottle that's good for two dollars off at the water park. We sell their product here. You see that big statue that's in the water park. This is a picture of it, with the man holding the Pepsi-Cola can. What happened was, when I bought that statue, that can was blank, and I went to both Coca-Cola and Pepsi-Cola to see how they would help us promote the water park, and Pepsi-Cola came up with the best deal. They not only paid us for that statue, but they put the coupon on the can. That's just in the state of New Jersey. They put two million of those out.

And Pepsi-Cola, the first hundred people into the park, they'll give one of these squeeze bottles to them on Tuesdays. On Thursdays, they have a shirt that has Water Park and Pepsi-Cola on the back. They give the first hundred people in here the shirts. And there's radio advertising that they do for us.

McDonalds sells, through their stores. I think we may have as many as twenty McDonalds this year selling tickets for us, which gives the people a dollar discount. Then, every time that one of those tickets come in, we donate a dollar to the Ronald McDonald House. Last year, we only had six or seven McDonalds in the area doing this, but we gave the Ronald McDonald House a check for five thousand dollars at the end of the year. McDonalds seemed to like that very much and they're thinking of expanding that up to twenty stores this year.

Then, Shoprite or Foodtown — one of the stores, I forget which one — is doing something with the coupons, their food coupons that they put out in the newspaper. They're putting out a coupon that would give a dollar off. And what we'll do for every one of those tickets that come in here, then we donate a dollar to the YMCA.

I think we have a great relationship with the community. I think they realize that we are the main attraction in town, and they cooperate with us in just about everything we do. Seaside used the carousel horse for the anniversary, [of the town] our fiftieth anniversary, maybe the seventy-fifth. The carousel horse was the motif. It doesn't bother me as an owner of the Casino Pier to advertise the town of Seaside Heights because I just feel if I get them into town, I'll get my share of the business.

In Islip, Long Island, Gerry Holzman and the Empire State Carousel also were successful with a raffle. Another of their achievements that might be emulated anywhere was involving continually more and more people in the carousel.

Bob Grauer of All County Amusements — God bless him — he donated the horse to be raffled off. It's a metal piece. It raised over a thousand dollars. The raffle will be the last Sunday before Christmas. We're going to raffle something else. We're going to have a perpetual raffle at all times. We find it's very nice. People come in, they want to buy a raffle ticket for a dollar, or five dollars, so we're going to have something to raffle all the time.

Finally, in 1984, the New York State legislature, at the request of my local assemblyman, passed a legislative resolution making us the unofficial official carousel of New York. As a little publicity got out, people sent us five dollars or ten dollars, but there was no money of any consequence.

Then, the following year, we got a grant from the New York State Council on the Arts, and that coupled with the money that Dick [Selchow] had given us, gave me courage and I took a year off, a leave of absence from my job, and I started to work on it. People started to get involved. We've sort of embodied a project we call the Tom Sawyer Project. Instead of three guys building a merry-go-round, other people got involved. And out of that came a variety of things. Came the bird carvings. They were donated by bird carvers, and they are still being donated by bird carvers all over the state. Song birds. The quilt project developed. We invited quilting clubs from all over the state to get involved and to contribute twenty-by-thirty inch quilt banners, depicting scenes from their region. The response to that has been overwhelming.

Our carving clubs from all over the state have carved frames, again depicting regional motifs. The Sullivan County Carvers chose the animals of the southern Catskills. The Long Island Carvers have clam shells and crabs, and a map of Long Island, harbor scenes and sailboats and such. We have twelve frames that have been carved.

We have wooden molding that's three inches wide, divided into sixteen-inch sections. We invited carvers from all over the state to carve the name of their community. Horseheads, Islip, Massapequa, Plattsburg, and a little design on the thing that would be appropriate to their community. Then, on the

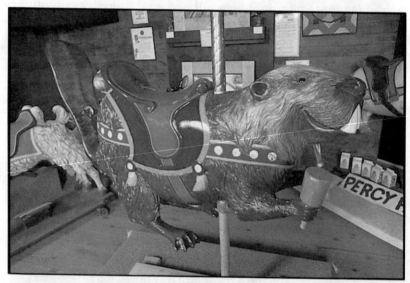

Figure 70. Bucky Beaver, the New York State animal, is to be the lead figure on the Empire State Carousel. Symbolically, he carries a set of woodcarving tools. It took Gerry Holzman two-hundred-seventy-five hours to carve Bucky Beaver. (Photo: Gerry Holzman)

Figure 71. As with all of the animals on the Empire State Carousel, Denny Deermouse is filled with symbolism. He was sponsored by the Natural Heritage Trust, so their name and a map of New York State is on the medallion. Denny Deermouse beats a drum because the deermouse is a nocturnal animal and is susposed to drum on the ground with his feet. The motto on the drum is the motto of New York State, *Excelsior,* which means "Ever upward." (Photo: Gerry Holzman)

bottom edge of the molding, we asked them to carve their name so that they can come to the carousel and point up to that piece of the molding and say, "That's mine." So that's where we're involving another hundred of our people.

It was not our carousel anymore. It's a carousel that's been carved by New Yorkers throughout the state. We have over seven hundred people at this point who have contributed creatively to the project, and our goal is to go over a thousand people. In many communities throughout New York state, there are people who can proudly say "That carousel is something that I helped to create."

We've invited high school students from all over New York state to paint scenes from their region. Two foot by three foot scenes of places like Niagara Falls or the Adirondacs. We have a built in insurance project with the idea of kids being involved in it. At least fifty or sixty years of interest right there. If a kid has done a painting in high school for

Figure 72. As well as symbolism, humor is abundant on the Empire State Carousel. Among the titles of the books carried by Freddie the Frog are: *Famous Frogs of New York*, with 1247 entries, and *Entymology, a Gourmet's Guide*. His flag reads "I love New York Bugs." (Photo: Gerry Holzman)

the carousel, he's going to have a vested interest in seeing that carousel preserved.

The idea of developing personal proprietary interest in a carousel is a concept that those responsible for the Broome County merry-go-rounds have achieved with wonderful results. Binghamton Cultural Affairs Director Toni Grekin tells how she and Gail Domin, Coordinator of the Urban Cultural Parks Program, made public awareness their priority.

> The first thing we felt we had to do before we even did nuts and bolts was to raise the consciousness of the community in terms of what a treasure they had rather than just taking them for granted. It's important to understand, we're in a valley and it's a fairly self-sufficient valley. The children in this community, and their parents, and their grandparents all grew up knowing that there were carousels here, but not understanding that on the other side of our mountain range or down river some other place, there was no such thing anymore. That from the four to six thousand carousels

Figure 73. Binghamton, New York, street horse "Glorious Black and White" by Richard Barons and family, Broome Community College. Ten "street horses" were placed on the main streets of downtown Binghamton to increase awareness of the historic Broome County carousels. (Photo: Ed Aswad, Carriage House Photography)

Figure 74. Two street horses on Court Street in Binghamton, New York, being enjoyed by visitors. (Photo: Ed Aswad, Carriage House Photography)

that were considered to have been in America and in Canada, we were down, at this point, to one hundred-seventy. Still intact. That doesn't mean one hundred-seventy operating carousels. The number operating, I believe, is lower than one hundred. So our kids didn't understand that this was something special. They go to a park and expect to see a carousel. And not only to see a carousel, but assume that it's free.

West Junior High School had a wonderful project. I believe it was in 1984. Two of the art teachers organized the kids to repaint them [the horses]. They did a loving job and there's no question that it was a wonderful opportunity to make them feel proprietary about the carousel. In fact, it was the beginning of the consciousness about the carousels.

I go to different schools in the community, and when I started this three years ago, [1987] I was surprising the children. We felt if the kids did not grow up cherishing them, they would never survive. So a special effort had to go into that. It couldn't just be, "Yes, we have carousels, isn't it nice?" You had to startle them.

We felt another thing that was critically important was the training session for all of the park employees that were going to run the carousels. We first thought "Aaahh, what do they care about history?" but they were just wonderful. Enthusiastic. Involved. We went through things like tours, like people might want to know how to get to the next park, so familiarize yourself. Stack the brochure rack. Listen to their problems. From that type of thing to sharing maintenance concerns, the different histories.

We have about two thousand kids that come through City Hall, and then I go out too. Now when I say to the kids, "What's special about Binghamton?" they say, "We have our carousels." So there's no question about it, the consciousness has been raised.

Ross Park has a gift shop for the park, in the carousel museum. People can adopt-a-horse at Ross Park and at Rec Park. And there is a local group that has formed for the restoration of all six carousels. "Friends of Our Carousels." We've done posters. We had shirts for the carousel run, which all sold out. We have the pin. I'm hoping with this private group that is now organized, the Friends of Our Carousels, that they can get into this more than we can. I don't think there's anyone locally, in the region, in the vicinity that doesn't know

162

Figure 75. The Carousel Museum at Ross Park. "Having that museum is a way of protecting the carousels. It's mostly carousel education. It raises consciousness" — Toni Grekin. (Photo: Ed Aswad, Carriage House Photography)

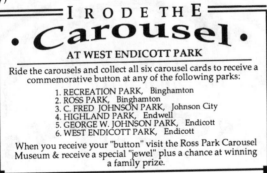

Figure 76. "Ride the Carousel Circuit" is a very popular program for promoting the Broome County carousels. Anyone who rides one of the six carousels receives a corresponding "I rode the carousel" card. After all six cards are collected, riders turn them in for a carousel button. The buttons can then be brought to the carousel museum at Ross Park to receive a special "jewel" and a chance at a family prize. The first year, one-thousand-thirty-seven people completed the circuit. In 1994, nearly four thousand people, representing almost every state, Canada, Europe and Australia, completed the circuit. (Courtesy Gail Domin)

163

about our carousels now. That we have six. Why they are important. How expensive they are to restore. So, from my perspective, with my program, it was definitely successful. Before, I don't think people really understood the importance or the value of the carousels.

Involving the community in the merry-go-round, especially the children, is one of the best ways to promote public awareness of the historical significance and beauty of carousels. In Martha's Vineyard, the children were part of the fund raising efforts to purchase the Flying Horses, the oldest operating carousel in the United States. As Executive Director of The Martha's Vineyard Historical Preservation Society, Jane Chittick made an arrangement with the then owner to run the carousel through the summer and try to raise the seven-hundred-and-fifty thousand dollar purchase price by the December deadline.

I had about five weeks in which to somehow staff a carousel and learn the whole business of it and everything else. Get it going, open to the public and start a fund raising cam-

Figure 77. The Fund for the Preservation of the Flying Horses logo is found on the postcards sold in the gift shop at the carousel in Martha's Vineyard. (Courtesy The Flying Horses Carousel Foundation, Inc.)

paign. That was in late April, 1986. We opened Memorial Day that year and we ran it open seven days a week, twelve hours a day. We ran it through Labor Day and then weekends until Columbus Day.

It was very difficult. I did a number of ads, actually beautiful ads, done by the *Vineyard Gazette*, lovely, just a frontal view of the horse and then I entitled it "Endangered Species." I described how it was a band of twenty horses that came to this island in 1884, and they had lived here ever since, and now they were in danger of leaving and disappearing, and it was up to everyone here to save them. And they did.

We also had organized a walk by the children to raise money. About three hundred or so children. That was done on Columbus Day. They got pledges and they raised ten thousand dollars in one day themselves.

We also devised a program to preserve a horse. We would approach certain individuals for corporate groups on the island, and for a twenty-five thousand dollar gift, they would have preserved an individual horse and have the right to name that horse. We were very successful with that. And then syndicates, groups got together, each giving a certain amount of money.

The horses were named by these various individuals, and we named others just from the general contributions given, but the lead horse we gave to the children. We said the children had preserved this horse, and we named it *Pegasus* after the first flying horse. The fact that *Pegasus* was eventually accorded a place of honor among the gods and found a permanent resting home we like to liken to the Flying Horses here.

To promote interest in and develop funds for restoration of their small carousel, Joyce Hanks and Jane Lee persuaded All Hallows Guild of the Washington National Cathedral to publish a coloring book and develop a cross stitch kit. The book, with drawings by Babs Gaillard, shows the animal figures with the Cathedral in the background and gives a brief history of the carousel which was manufactured more than a hundred years ago by the US Merry-Go-Round Company. In addition to the coloring book, Joyce Hanks and Jane Lee described their other promotional endeavors.

All Hallows Guild does have a gift shop, that's the Herb Cottage right there on the grounds, and they sell all kinds of gifts. Over a period of time, we've developed things for the merry-go-round. I found Alice DiCaprio, who's a great carousel enthusiast and artist, and I started buying little pins from her. Parker pony pins that were very popular. And then, we came out with our own coloring book. Actually, we've printed it three times now, and each time it's gotten larger and more interesting. Then last year, since it was the one hundredth anniversary, we developed a counted cross stitch kit. A Centennial commemorative counted cross stitch kit with one of our restored animals on it. So we do market a few things.

We have not learned how to market things terribly well, and we'll learn that over a period of time. But meeting some

ALL HALLOWS GUILD OF WASHINGTON NATIONAL CATHEDRAL

THE CAROUSEL CLUB COLORING PAD,
Illustrated by Babs Gaillard

Figure 78. An All Hallows Guild project to raise funds for the restoration of their carousel is the coloring book illustrated by Babs Gaillard. The 1995 copy and fourth edition, which portrays the changes in the restored figures, depicts all twenty-two animals, two sleighs, and the caliola. (Courtesy Joyce Hanks)

different carousel people, directors of organizations throughout the country, at that technical conference [NCA] in North Carolina last March, several of them were interested in what we had, and they did buy wholesale from us. So that was the first time we've marketed like that. It's something that's growing very slowly. There was an article in *Carousel News and Trader* a year ago, and we received fifty mail orders for our new coloring book. Two from overseas, from Germany and from Holland.

Now my whole family is interested in carousels. There is now going on a coloring contest using our carousel coloring book. Every family group has the coloring book and they're entering the coloring contest. So everyone, there are three year olds up to seventy, is entering the carousel coloring contest.

My sister lost her husband a couple of years ago, and just to help her recover, I invited her to come down from New York state to help me at "Flower Mart," and she loved it. So then, she came last year again, and she said, "Wouldn't it be nice to have a deer restored?" Well, the doe deer was restored and she's adorable. Her name's "Raspberry." At any rate, my sister and her children are now underwriting a restoration of the buck reindeer in memory of her husband. They live in the Adirondacks area so a reindeer is very appropriate. We'll dedicate that at our "Flower Mart" celebration. "Blackberry" in memory of Ned Merrell.

We had a grant from a private foundation, who underwrote the restoration of our two sleighs and a new vinyl top. It's just beautiful. It has been fun to get this interest in it going and see the response coming.

We brought out some post cards and we also had histories printed up, which we hand out to people standing in line waiting to get on the merry-go-round at "Flower Mart." You give the adults something to do while they're waiting. There's nothing lovelier than a day at the Cathedral on one of the beautiful days of "Flower Mart" to see all of the people there surrounded by flowers and by colors and all of the young families with their little tots. They arrive in beautiful little dresses and suits and so forth, and half an hour later they've cotton candy all over their faces. But it's just dear and that too is part of the spiritual side of it, the nurturing

Figure 79. The elephant named "Spirit" was restored and dedicated in 1992, in memory of Lee Atwater, Jr., former chairman of the Republican National Committee, who died of cancer at age forty-two. Each restoration on the carousel is dedicated to the memory of a person, and symbols reflecting the interests of that person are worked into the trappings and saddle blankets of the animals. (Photo: Karen Smith)

of families. We have third generation riders now on this carousel.

In October, actually the last day of September, we have Open House at the Cathedral, and it's too expensive to bring out the carousel, but we do bring out the caliola, and the elephant because he's easy for the children to sit on. There's always a crowd around the caliola, watching it, trying to figure out how it plays, and that sort of thing. That again stimulates interest for "Flower Mart" in the spring.

A carousel horse has become a logo for "Flower Mart" as well, and is used in their publicity and their handouts and so forth. Only, I would say, in the last twelve years has anything much been done to it because that's about the time there was this ground swell of interest throughout the United States in carousels. Bit by bit we have learned what we have. We didn't even know what we had or how unique it was. That's one of the reasons we wrote up these little histories that we use as handouts at "Flower Mart" to educate people to this special carousel that we are running for their benefit.

Figure 80. The Wurlitzer caliola that accompanies All Hallows Guild's merry-go-round is one of six made by Wurlitzer with brass pipes. The paintings were restored by the Nation's Capital Chapter of the National Society of Decorative Painters. The top medallion depicts the Herb Cottage, which is the gift shop of All Hallows Guild, and the lower medallion depicts the cathedral. (Photo: Karen Smith)

Posting signs on the merry-go-round itself or handing out brochures explaining the historical significance of their carousels are strategies used by many of the narrators to educate the public. Dr. Floyd Moreland in Seaside Heights, New Jersey, explains his efforts to make people aware of their antique Dentzel/Looff carousel.

> What we tried to do — after we redid a lot of it — was to have signs made, which you'll see posted in the building, about the historical significance. Signs telling that it dates back to 1910, that the animals are all hand carved, and please respect it. Of course, we give out the little flyer at the shop, and people have responded incredibly. They read it. Even sometimes when people are fooling around when the ride's moving. If I tell them, "Please read the sign," or I'll tell them a little bit about the machine. Nine times out of ten they become very passive, and they start looking. And when it's over, they go for a flyer and they read it. So, I believe that with all of these signs, which are rather unique in the country, I believe we're educating people. It is true the abuse level has gone down in the past three years on this machine. It exists, it always will. There will always be someone who won't care, but it's gone down considerably. And the ridership has gone up.

> I feel privileged [to be running the carousel at Seaside Heights] as I think not only am I enjoying myself and doing something I've always wanted to do, but I think I'm making a contribution in general. In some ways, it's as important, and maybe more important, than the contribution I make as a college professor. I think I reach more people. Teaching Greek and Latin, you instill values of the past, and you preserve the past in one way. In doing this, I'm doing something very similar. It's a more recent past. I think I'm reaching larger numbers so I'm still the educator, seven days a week.

> If you went to fiberglass, you would have the frame left, but then it would be just an amusement ride, which will bring you joy and a lot of fun to people. But that sense of the past and that thread that connects us with the present and the future is gone. And the personalities of the individuals who created these, that's gone. It's as if you take the life out of it.

Of course I'm prejudiced, but I think this is the nicest carousel that I've ever seen. There are many carousels that are far more ornate.

I think — and this I can say with some objectivity — I think this carousel is one of the best maintained. That's not because I'm involved in this. People say that all the time. A lot of people say — this warms me a great deal — they say, when they look at this when it's turning, they say, they can see there's love that goes into this carousel.

9

Household Hints

The people most closely connected with running and maintaining carousels, through experience or experiment, have discovered novel or different ways of doing their job. Their trade secrets and suggestions are presented here to help save time, work, and money. Some of these short cuts and hints may be familiar to readers who also are involved in carousel operations. Many of the ideas may have people wondering, "Now why didn't I think of that?" and all are worthy of consideration since they are suggestions that have proven to be useful by those who know. As Conservation Chairman of the National Carousel Association, Charles Walker prepared several brochures on carousel maintenance and operation. These highly informative booklets are available to anyone involved with carousel operation and can be obtained through the National Carousel Association. In his interview, Charles explained how he learned through doing and came up with several ideas not yet incorporated into the brochures.

My father, meantime, became ill and passed away, but his thought before he passed away was to get a small merry-go-round that was in working order so that I could operate that and make enough money to fix the big one. Well, that's not very good thinking because the little carousel that I bought I take that out to parties and occasions, and it all fits

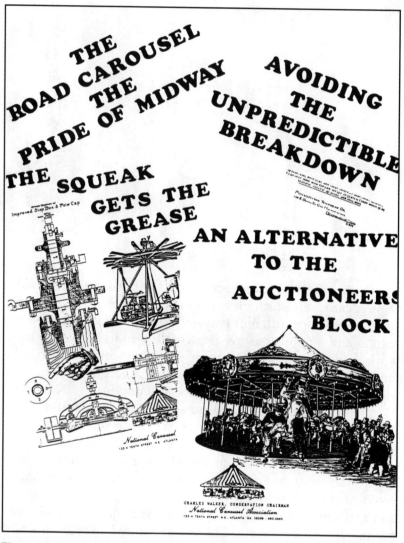

Figure 81. Charles Walker, Conservation Chairman of the National Carousel Association, prepared several technical leaflets that promote keeping and maintaining existing carousels rather than sending them to the auction block. These leaflets are available without charge from the National Carousel Association. (Photo: Courtesy Charles Walker)

in the truck so that's handy, but there's no way to raise enough money operating a carousel to fix another carousel.

I picked up a lot of experience moving the little one around. They say that three men in six hours can install the little one.

Take it out of the truck and put it together. I think most of those men must have died doing it because I can't find three men that can do it. Every time you get around one of these machines you learn something new. Of course, I've learned an enormous amount by working on this one. I've picked up a lot about operation and how things ought to be along the way because I had to learn and pick it up from those who have gone on before. I'm still learning. It's a learning process, and I've had to update a lot of my little brochures. Every year that I go to the [International Association of Amusement Parks] convention, we give out in the neighborhood of two or three hundred of each one of the items that I have printed. I have about six. They are good reading material for anybody whose interested in carousels and how to make them run better, and how to make money with them. I need to do one on where to put one. I'm trying to figure that out right now so if I discover it, then I'm going to write that up.

One thing that I just learned in the past year — some person in the amusement business — I said the brass was almost impossible to polish, that some of it would just turn black, and it was just hard to polish, and they said, "Well, the trick is to use toilet bowl cleaner and bicarbonate of soda, and it just comes right off." And sure enough, that's one of the best brass polishers I've ever seen. Of course, it's a little bit caustic, but it takes that tarnish off.

So, you learn these little helpful hints like that. If your clutch slips, you know to put talcum powder in it to soak up the grease, or you put corn starch in it. That's another thing to soak up the grease.

Running the carousel is a very hard job to see that each one of the customers, every five or six minutes has the perfect performance from your production. The band organ, of course, is very repetitious. It will guarantee to draw a crowd anywhere, but, nevertheless, most of 'em play in the same key all day long, and it gets very monotonous, and the help doesn't want to stay with you. They can't stand the repetition of that. When you have a big machine like this, it's always good to have a variety of music and that way you don't get bored. You can change over.

With the liabilities and everything, I think that you need to charge at least a dollar to ride. That's kind of unheard of to the old timers who used to pay a nickel to ride. But you've got to understand that the local bread has gone up. I advise everybody never to charge more for a ride on a carousel than a box of popcorn. Now popcorn is going for $1.00–$1.25 so I'm right on with that, being as popcorn is eighty-five percent profit.

[Buying carousel figures] certainly is not a very good investment unless you really love the animal as much as you pay for it. I would just advise not putting money into carousel horses unless they're on a machine where it can gather some revenue.

These brochures that I pass out sort of cheer people on who have old carousels. They think that it's old, it's been in their park, it needs to be done away with and get a new one because that's the attitude of the people who make the new ones. And they don't give a thought to the fact that the thing has been there for fifty, sixty, seventy years running faithfully, and it needs to have a little fluffing up. So, I should think, after fifty or sixty years, you would want to take it apart and work on it a little bit, and then it will be good for another fifty or sixty years.

Some of the carousels that are being made out of fiberglass even have the old look because that's one of the things that I have been harping on. That, if you're going to have an old carousel, it should look like an old carousel, and not a new, modern, up-to-date carousel with fluorescent lights so that it looks like somebody's kitchen.

Most of the companies that are making fiberglass carousels right now will guarantee their animals for one season, and rightfully so, because fiberglass begins to get brittle. The place that gives away is right through the middle of the horse. There is a company in Mansfield, Ohio, that will guarantee their wood horses for five years. I daresay that after five years, they would last another fifty. No problem. Wood is very durable and very lasting. The old boys were right. You can pile tons of weight on a wood horse and it will hold it up. You pile tons of weight on a fiberglass horse and the inside rips out and it just won't hold up.

You can buy bass wood today, and you can have brand new carousel horses made out of wood just the same way the old guys did it. Some of the people are realizing that the wood for new horses is as inexpensive as fiberglass. Three thousand you can get a wood horse, brand new.

Figure 82. "I should think, after fifty or sixty years, you would want to take it apart and work on it a little bit, and then it will be good for another fifty or sixty years" — Charles Walker. (Photo: Courtesy Charles Walker)

Anyone thinking of purchasing an antique carousel figure should take collector Charlotte Dinger's warning seriously.

I think anybody who collects today has to be extremely careful that they are dealing with somebody who's reputable. I'm getting letters and phone calls from people who are buying reproductions without knowing it. They're being told that they're antiques, and there are some disreputable people who are very smart about how to make a horse look old. They take the animal to a stripping place and have it partially stripped. They leave some paint on and take some paint off and the wood shows through in spots. Then they put the animals out of doors for about six weeks, in the rain, snow,

Figure 83. "Buyer Beware" is the motto when shopping for a carousel figure. Some reproductions look very much like authentic figures. (Photo: Carrie Papa)

sleet, it doesn't matter. And the wood ages. People are being fooled. The wood starts to crack and split. It turns gray and the paint's rubbed off and they say, "Oh, this definitely is old," but it might have been carved in Spain or Mexico a few months before. So, it's a real problem in collecting today.

If you're prepared to do a lot of work and you enjoy woodworking, and you have a great deal of patience, it's wonderful to buy a horse that needs a lot of attention. There's a great deal of satisfaction in seeing something come back to the way it should be. When you buy it and it's in pieces and has dry rot and all that, there's a great deal of pleasure in restoring an animal to its original glory.

Many people have purchased "basket cases" that need a lot of restoration and possibly even some new carving. Others are carving their own carousel animals from scratch. In either case, anyone who will be doing carving should heed the recommendation of master carver Kenneth Lynch.

Buy the best tools that you can possibly afford. The first set of tools that I ever bought, it came in a set and being a novice, I just didn't realize that you don't look to save money for a good tool. You look to spend as much as you possibly can. If you can't afford a good one, don't buy something that's second-rate because it just doesn't work. Debbie's father [narrator's father-in-law] that was one of the first things that he ever told me. He said, "Don't buy tools unless you can afford the best." It really has proved to be true.

As I said before, there's thousands of different shapes and sizes. You don't need thousands in order to be able to do good work. But you do need good quality tools in order to do good work.

[To be] a carver you really just have to carve, and carve, and carve. The more you do, the more proficient you get — if you have the talent to begin with. I think it was Edison who said that genius is ninety-nine percent perspiration and one percent inspiration. I think that holds true to carving too.

However, before purchasing an expensive set of carving tools and starting in on a full-size carousel animal, prospective carvers are advised to start with a small project first. While one never knows where an X-acto carving set might lead, at least the cost is not too prohibitive an investment. For Gerry Holzman, his first set of carving tools eventually led to the Empire State Carousel.

My mother always gives me a Christmas present. This particular year, 1971, she called me up and said, "What do you want for Christmas?" I happened to have the *New York Times* open to the Shoppers Guide in the back, and there at the bottom it said "X-acto Carving Sets, $7.95." So, I told her what I wanted was an X-acto Carving Set for Christmas. And I told her exactly the number and such and that's what she sent me, a little X-acto Carving Set.

I experimented a little. I've always had an affinity for wood. I was attracted to wood carvings. And for two or three years, I did things with the X-acto. I made myself a chess set. I made some little animal carvings. I bought a few books and I joined the National Woodcarvers Association. Subscribed to their magazine called *Chip Chats*. I got pretty good, but I was really a folk carver more than anything else.

Then, we spent a good part of the summer in England. I built the trip around visiting wood carvers. I had gotten a list of them from *Chip Chats* magazine. I visited Gino Masero, who is one of the thirty-two master carvers left in England. There was a certain chemistry and he and I hit it off quite well. He was old enough to be my father almost, I guess, but we just got along very well. When we came home, I sent him a little gift, and we exchanged letters and such.

Then, in the spring of that year, I got the idea that maybe I could become his pupil, so I wrote and asked if he would take me on for a week as a student, and he agreed. So, that Easter vacation, I flew over to England, and Gino put all of his work aside, and I spent the week working with him. He raised my consciousness. He showed me what a good carver could do. I realized how inadequate my attempts had been at this point. And though, he didn't improve my skills dramatically that time, he made me aware of what was possible. He showed me how to sharpen my tools, which I'd never known how to do. He divorced me from the X-actos. I went on to gouges and chisels. He took me to a number of carving shops and I bought a set of tools. He said, "Go home and come back next year." Which is what I did. I worked on the projects that he gave me. I sent him letters and photographs and he critiqued them. The following spring I came back. This time, with a project that I wanted to do. I did that for six years. Going over and working with Gino. That sort of got me to the point where I understood. I learned how to carve. Certainly in six weeks you don't learn how to become a master carver, but with six weeks spread out over six years, that made quite a difference.

I had been now carving about ten years, and a friend of mine, Bruno Speiser, sold me my first carousel horse. A real beat up Parker western with a lariat, pistol, on the side and such, and it was in terrible condition. The condition of sale that Bruno gave me was, "If you buy it, I'll teach you how to restore it." He was as good as his word. He taught me how to restore the carousel horses, just the way Gino taught me to love the curved line and to love quality carving. Bruno taught me to love the carousel. So, I am indebted to those two enormously.

Bruno and I became very good friends. We still are to this day. We went off on many a carousel horse hunting expedition, he and I, and I began restoring old horses under his tutelage. Then, I branched out on my own. Picked up a number of horses, restored them, sold them. Developed my own collection and such. This all went on, and I guess it was 1983, almost everything seemed to make me ready for this. I had the background in carousels. I had the background in restoration. I had the background in carving. I had an extremely rich depository to draw from so I created the concept of the Empire State Carousel.

Several of the narrators stressed the importance of cleanliness in running a successful operation. Keeping a park clean, with everything looking bright and new, was a fundamental idea that was repeated more than once. Edward Lange believes that cleanliness and annual upgrading contributed a great deal to the long success of Palace Amusements in Asbury Park, New Jersey.

I stress cleanliness. To have everything running properly. To have the place as clean as possible. Always stress cleanliness. Of course, the rides you have to maintain, paint them and fix them up so they look fresh. Which, more or less, is

Figure 84. The brass poles on PTC #84 were polished daily while it was at Palisades Amusement Park. (Photo: Courtesy Richard Scheiss)

what Disney does. Of course, we're a little peanut compared to Disney. You know when you go to Disney, or you've heard probably, cleanliness, cleanliness. Do you know at Disney, every night they have crews of people to touch up, paint. They clean and they paint, every night. That's the stress, cleanliness. You see people picking up all the time. We always did. Very important. We had one man, that's all he did every day. Pick up.

We paid great attention to adding different gadgets. New things used to come out so we would always try to upgrade everything. Trying to improve. Every year you had to improve. You had to find something new. We sold rides. We bought rides. We changed rides. We added machines every year. Bought new equipment. Arcade machines. They came out with more sophisticated machines every year. The arcade machines. You had to constantly upgrade. Always. Always. Always. You never could stand still. And move things around a little to make the place look different. The same as stores do it. They move things around, you know. So, you can never stand still. You have to keep changing.

Paul Woehle, owner of Fairy Tale Forest in Oakridge, New Jersey, also emphasized the importance of keeping things clean and in good working order. And, he was emphatic about the value of closing early in the evening.

We keep everything neat and clean. You've got to keep it clean. That's the most important thing. If something needs to be done, the township knows we are going to take care of it, and we do. We run it right.

This is a family place. This is for families with little kids. We have kids that come about eight or ten years, twelve years. We don't want the big crowds here. That's how we keep it. Nursery school to about third grade as far as groups go. It's a strictly family business. They bring their little babies and everything. Up to two years, we don't charge. And they all like it. I met a doctor there once. He came in with a little boy on his hand and he wanted to go on the merry-go-round. He says, "You know, I have to tell you something. When I came here the first year, I was his size. Now I come and bring my little boy." That's what family business is. It's repeating.

I always got new ideas. I make something new here. Always something new. The next thing — I'm working on it for a couple of years already — it will be finished this year. The Rain Tree. It's like a little humor scene. You see a little house in a tree there on a hill, and you see a gorilla in there and he's eating bananas. He's moving around. I bought him, and he looks too gruesome so I stick a big banana in his mouth and he's got a couple bananas in his hand.

We keep the price to go in very low. It's more an amusement for the people, that's why we keep it very low. We open ten o'clock in the morning. Six o'clock we close. I saw down at the seashore, the parks there. It was beautiful. Then they started to open nights and that was the finish of Asbury Park. That was beautiful there. Then they started nights and they got the riffraff there. That's why we close up early. We don't want it nights. Everybody likes it. Everybody. I always say Fairy Tale Forest put Oak Ridge on the map because we are right in the Esso map, right in there.

Another respondent who believed in keeping the price low was David Gillian who dates back to when a ride on the merry-go-round was a nickel.

I was working when a nickel wasn't too bad to have. I have always run for five cents, six for a quarter. And I kept that price all the time I was there. So, finally, they opened up a place right on this corner. Man that's got this big department store, Stainton. He come up to me one time, and said, "Mr. Gillian," he says, "You ought to raise your merry-go-round to ten cents." So, I got talking to him, and I says, "Mr. Stainton, do you have a bargain counter in your store?" He says, "Yes." I said, "Well, that's my bargain counter on the beach. So, I'm staying five cents, six for a quarter."

It stayed that way until I quit. This makes about seventy-three years in Ocean City, I guess. I come in 1914. I've made it my life. Playing music was a sideline, but the merry-go-round was always my best interest. I was very nice with the public. With the kiddies especially. I think I gave out many, many thousands of tickets to the people. My wife sometimes, in the evening, would set on the bench around the merry-go-round. I had all benches around. And some little girls would be around her. And my wife had tickets in her pocketbook. I always say, that was my advertisement. So the little kiddies would come up — she'd be setting on the bench there — "I wish I could get another ride. I don't have another ticket." Then, my wife would give her a ticket, and say, "Now

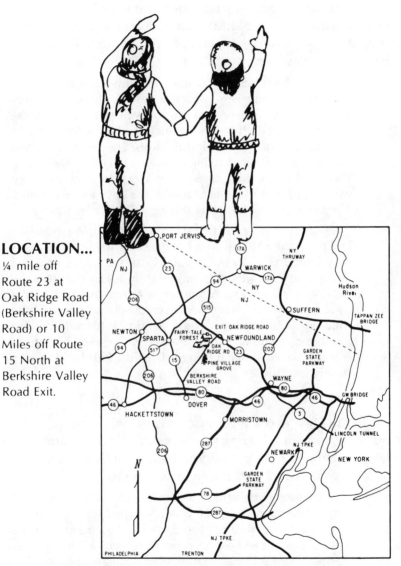

LOCATION...
¼ mile off Route 23 at Oak Ridge Road (Berkshire Valley Road) or 10 Miles off Route 15 North at Berkshire Valley Road Exit.

Figure 85. "I always say Fairy Tale Forest put Oak Ridge on the map because we are right in the Esso map, right in there" — Paul Woehle.

185

will you go right home and go to bed?" So, I was always very sociable and my wife was a just right wonderful girl. Wonderful.

A practical business suggestion involves keeping the carousel separate from the kiddie rides. Raymond D'Agostino used this strategy at Bertrand Island Amusement Park in Lake Hopatcong, New Jersey.

> Back in the fifties, they came out with what they called kiddie rides. They were miniature rides for little children of ages anywhere from a year old to five years old. Only the kids could get on them. No adults. We had, at one time in our park, we had twelve kiddie rides. They were all in one section. A lot of them had big umbrellas over the top of them. There were little pony carts. There were fire engines. There were little boats that went around in a big water enclosure. They were all just little tiny things, a Ferris wheel.
>
> We did not allow a little minature carousel. We didn't allow that in the kiddie land because that would have naturally interfered with our regular carousel. So we kept our carousel apart, in its own building by itself. That was the carousel for anybody. A mother or father that had a little child. They would stand on the carousel and put the little child on the horse. They would stand next to the horse and go around and around. The carousel was for everybody from any age from one to a hundred. The little kiddie rides were strictly for children.

For the few existing carousel owners who still use the ring machine, and find the rings both expensive to buy and hard to keep on hand, the means devised by Roy Gillian and his family to reduce costs and theft might be of interest.

> We go through them like you can't believe. This year, [1989] for the first year, Campbell Chain stopped selling them direct to us. We go through about, oh maybe a hundred gross a year. I spent maybe over three thousand dollars in rings this year because I had to buy them through a retailer. The price went up tremendously. What happened this year, or so I was told, Campbell Chain up in Pennsylvania, in Erie,

all their supply of rings was being used by Exxon up on the oil spill. Now whether that's a true story or not, I don't know. But, at least that's what they told us.

There are a certain amount of people that ride it just for that. It's just something that I think is part of it. People take the rings for souvenirs. I don't know what it is. They walk away. They're not all brass rings. They are just the regular rings. It's funny. I remember back during the war time years, we had trouble getting them. We used to go down and put them in a bucket of salt water and rust them up a little bit before we used them, so that they wouldn't take them. Back in those days, we had a hard time getting them. It sounds like you're a cheapie to do that, but it was just one of those things you had to do at the time.

If paying for expensive rings just to see them disappear as souvenirs is a problem, perhaps the device invented by Robert Long for the Eldridge Park carousel presents an alternative. Scott Bittler describes his grandfather's invention.

Figure 86. The electronic brass ring feeder designed by Robert Long was the only one in the country. One brass ring per ride would drop as riders hit the right combination of lights on the electronic board. (Photo: The Chemung County Historical Society, Elmira, New York)

Gosh, I don't remember what year it was that we had to change the way we operated that [the ring machine] because as ring feeders on merry-go-rounds across the country became scarcer due to insurance problems and so forth, it became very expensive. Another problem cropped up which was that they became great souvenir items and people kept them. All of them, not just the brass rings, but the iron rings as well. You know, you're operating a ride with a ticket price that's very low, and it became a very expensive proposition.

So, the operation was changed on the ring machine to be that of just the brass ring. Whenever the brass ring wasn't there to be caught, you would simply be clicking the fingers on the ring feeder. Then, a new device was added. Again, invented by my grandfather. It was an electronic device that had a big light board, a matrix of lights hanging from the ceiling that could be seen from the location of the feeder. As you went through and clicked the fingers on the feeder, the lights would change. So, it was just a little visual response to your clicking of the fingers that would kind of keep you occupied.

It operated that way up through the time when we stopped the operation of the ride. It's the only one of it's kind that I'm aware of anywhere. There was one copy of the electronics, I think, made at one time for either the Rochester or Easton branches of the Long family, but I don't know that it was actually deployed in either of those locations. But the way this would work is the lights would kind of keep the riders occupied with the machine until — typically once or twice per ride — the operator of the machine where they had the controls, would push the button and that would trigger a brass ring to come down.

10

A Tremendous Quality and Charm

Nearly all of the narrators tried to define the enduring appeal of the merry-go-round. Most found this appeal had an elusive quality that could not be reduced to any one thing. Everyone found several reasons to account for one or another engaging features of the carousel. Dr. Floyd Moreland considers the historical aspect to explain the magic.

> In the very early stages of carousels in this country, most of them were in what was known as trolley parks. They were owned by the people who owned trolley companies and they were placed at the end of the line to encourage people to come out there, particularly on a weekend. To buy the land and so forth. Real estate developers would support them, and in those days, as I understand from history, they were part of a social event. You would go on a Sunday afternoon to the end of the trolley line. You'd picnic. You'd ride the carousel, and it was a big thing.
>
> Can you imagine, just think for a moment, the-turn-of-the-century, people living in an urban setting, most being immigrants. America's supposed to be paved with gold, but it's not quite that way. Life is hard, maybe not having electricity, certainly not having phonographs or radios. Then you take a trolley, and at the end of it, there's this marvelous thing. Colors, animals, lights, music, mechanical music with

drums beating, and, sometimes on fancier organs than ours, little figures turning around leading bands and stuff. That must have been absolutely thrilling for people who were struggling in their own lives. It's sort of a glimpse of the world of tomorrow. Sort of a pastoral freedom and beauty in these animals prancing happily with all this electricity around it. I try to think back at the perspective, how people then must have felt when they perceived something like this, and it had to be sheer magic.

[Today] the magic is there in another sense, though it's still in the dreams. There's something. I can't put my finger on it, but I see it in children and I see it in older people. In the middle it's missing.

Children talk to them a great deal. There is no other ride, no other mechanical object, I think, that captures the imagination of children so much. I see kids whisper in their ears. They wave hello and goodbye. It's just incredible. That is part of the eternal magic, and the dreams that these machines can generate.

When you run a carousel, one takes the tickets while it's moving normally, and you walk against it, facing the animals. These animals all have glass eyes. They're all imported from Europe, as they were in those days, and the eyes are all different. They look at you, and there are different expressions, and it's quite interesting. And I'm not the nutty professor talking here. I mean other people, carousel operators and such, share this kind of thing. Quite different from the fiberglass animals that you see on more contemporary machines where the personality is not there. This is my favorite horse. You have to look at him to understand. He's just got a personality, a warmth, the smile. There's something very inviting about him.

At Central Park in New York, you'll see men in three piece suits, policemen, you see a very interesting crowd of people in the middle of the day. I always find that fascinating, because what a lot of them are doing is unwinding. It's fascinating. If you go around that carousel sometime at lunch time, you see the people, all alone, professional looking and cops, just sitting on a horse riding around. I think the people in Central Park stand back and reflect. I can see it in the older people. They look at each other, and you can see in their eyes that they are going through a time warp. You can just tell that something very special is happening as they ride. It's quite remarkable. Operate a merry-go-round for one day and you'll see what I mean.

Right now, in the season that we're in, mostly we have families. Young families with children, and lots of adults, fifties, sixties and up. In the summertime, more little kids vacationing, and of course lots of teenagers. But, I guess, to generalize, it's little children with their parents. As they grow older

Figure 87. "They look at you, and there are different expressions" — Floyd L. Moreland. (Photo: Courtesy George W. Long)

then alone, and older people. And, of course, little tiny babies. The baby doesn't know what's going on and frequently is afraid, but you can see in their fathers — more and more fathers than mothers, I think — you can see in the father's eyes that this is a very special moment. That he's introducing his child to a carousel. As it turns, I like to watch the eyes of people. There is something very special about it.

Probably the emotional appeal of the merry-go-round, the nostalgic delight of a return to childhood, is what the majority of adults most appreciate when thinking of a carousel. However, a collector of carousel figures like Charlotte Dinger admires the carvings as works of art and responds with a more esthetic view.

Our country produced the most beautiful carousels in the world. The operators and owners of carousels didn't know what they had. The thing you would hear most often is, "It's a German carousel." I eventually learned that they weren't German. Most were made in America. Even though the carousel started in Europe, The European animals, particularly the English animals, are very stiff and box-like. They don't have the fluid beauty of the American animals. Immigrants, who became carousel owners, had backgrounds in carving. One carved decorations for palaces, one carved wooden combs, and others made cabinets and furniture. American carvers developed a freer style because carousels were going into permanent locations. In Europe, they traveled the fair grounds. From week to week they would move. So, patterns were limited. The animals' poses were stiffer for easy stacking and moving. Whereas, the American park carousel animals had a variety of leg positions and heads in different poses. There was more freedom of artistic expression allowed. That's why the animals are so much lovelier than the other figures of the world.

With all the confusion of a carousel ride, one doesn't have time to study the animals. But a museum exhibition provides you the opportunity to see a cherub on the side of a horse or a lion. Many visitors say, "I never noticed those carvings before. Aren't they wonderful." It would be a shame not to preserve these wonderful sculptures. I've seen carousel animals held together with ropes. The bodies were actually falling apart. The glue had loosened and the seams had split. They were out of doors without a proper cover. They were not protected and the carousel was not supervised well. I think in cases of neglect it is right for collectors to spend their time, effort, and money restoring the figures. Because they would have been lost forever — many have been lost through the years.

It's important that exhibitions awaken public interest in preserving carousels. I like sharing the animals, and have had over twenty museum shows including the Baltimore Museum of Art and a large traveling show beginning in New York sponsored by the Museum of American Folk Art. The animals traveled as far west as Michigan and then down to North Carolina and up to New England. A lot of people enjoyed these exhibits. I've received letters and phone calls from people who say they brought back so many wonderful memories of their childhood. It's the type of show that appeals to all ages because the children enjoy the lions and the sea monsters and the unusual animals, and the older people are sure that the horse they're seeing is one that they rode as a child.

The carousel is a magical experience. It's one of your first adventures as a child. It's exciting. Your imagination soars. You can be a princess or a knight in armor, and you're on your own on this big horse or animal. I think everybody has fond memories of the carousel. People are smiling and all ages enjoy it. It's a happy experience recalling the joyful innocence of childhood.

Two other respondents equated the enjoyment of the carousel to a musical show or theatrical experience. Charles Walker in Atlanta feels that the carousel:

> ...is like a show. The lights have to be right. The speed has to be right. The music has to be right. It's like putting on a production for every person that rides.

They'll never build anything as elaborate as these grand old machines anymore. The machine has the thrill about it. There's something in the cranks. There's something in the mechanism. It's not just a wood horse or a plastic horse. It's the way it's constructed. It's the diameter. There's a lot of

Figure 88. City Park carousel, New Orleans, Louisiana. "People are smiling and all ages enjoy it" — Charlotte Dinger. (Photo: C. Dietz)

things to consider about the wooden ones. And, you realize that wood is real. There's so little real left in the world.

I hope that there will still be some carousels out there to be able to ride. And the children will be able to have the same grand thrill of being able to ride the wonderful old machines with oil paintings like the thrill that I got with a big band organ. There's just nothing that will compare to that kind of thrill of being on a piece of machinery that is fifty or sixty feet across and have that many horses on it and have the kind of acoustics that are in a big old rambling building. There's not an experience like that anywhere, and there are very few left in the country even with the ones that are being saved. You very seldom have that smell of old grease and years of what I consider integrity. There's a lot of carousels around, but there are very few carousels that have integrity. That's not new and shiny and fixed up. That's old and weathered nicely like an old oil painting.

In Binghamton, New York, to raise public awareness of the treasure they have in the six Broome County carousels, Gail

Domin and Toni Grekin arranged to have a dance troupe put on a Carousel Dance.

We are very fortunate to have a dance troupe in the local region. American Dance Asylum that does what they call "environmental dancing" or "interpretive dancing." The woman responsible, Lois Wilde, has taken pieces of architecture, buildings, or whatever and developed a dance per-

Figure 89. In addition to the carousel dance, Binghamton's Pops on the River picked up the merry-go-round theme with their floating carousel and *papier-mâché* horses. (Photo: Ed Aswad, Carriage House Photography)

formance around them based on their history and stuff. She did a pavilion dance with the big band era and then they decided to do a carousel dance.

It started with a very brief slide show with George F. Johnson with some of the old carousels. And some closeups of the carving, just the teeth, or the bridle, or something just to get you aware. They like to say a carousel has four art forms. There's the music. There's the carving, the sculpture of the figures. There's the painting involved in it. And there's the motion of the moving machine. And so, it's a very unique form of art when you combine all of those things. I think that was the purpose of the carousel dance, to make people aware of all of those things.

The way this worked was, the audience rode the carousel and the dance was performed around you. There were actually some people on the carousel that at certain times got off and danced around, hopping on and off. And then, the New York City dancers that came up were dressed as carousel

Binghamton, NY

Figure 90. Spectators line the banks of the Chenango River in mid-city Binghamton, New York, for this annual event that features the Binghamton City Pops Orchestra performing from a raft. A floating carousel emphasizes Broome County's unofficial title as the "Carousel Capital" of New York. (Photo: Ed Aswad, Carriage House Photography)

figures, horses and stuff, and they actually danced with the people. It was just beautiful.

Around the carousel at one spot there was a little vignette. There was a little scene, a Victorian kind of scene. It started with a little girl playing with a rocking horse. As the carousel went around, no matter what was happening with the dancing, every so often that little girl did a turn-around with a little older girl, and was replaced by her and the younger one disappeared. Then you went around a few more times, and she became a young woman. Then an older woman, and, finally, a very, very elderly lady sitting in a rocking chair. Then, she was replaced again by a younger child, a younger girl and so it was real goose bump stuff in terms of the circle of life and the movement of the carousel. The music was magnificent based on the sound of the carousel music, but it was an original piece. It was to cry from, that beautiful.

So again, there was this constant reaching out to the community. Again, it was that we have something special. Between "EJ" [Endicott Johnson] having the one hundredth anniversary and what we've done with the carousels, and what they're starting to see. The carousel is such an easy and tangible focus and friendly reminder to people of the specialness of their past and why it's important to continue it.

Most of the narrators could not limit the appeal of the merry-go-round to any two or three aspects. The historical significance was an important element to several, and to others the art form itself was dominant. To Gerry Holzman, community involvement and an awareness of ones cultural heritage were prominent factors in determining the purpose of the Empire State Carousel.

The reason I'm building a carousel is — I've sat down and I've tried to analyze them and I can't. There's just an enormous number. I remember taking a history course once on the Middle East, and someone said, "What is the problem in the Middle East?" Some fellow got up and answered, "The problem in the Middle East is the Middle East, and there are a hundred different facets to it."

One is very selfish. As I said before, it's the grandest thing a wood carver can do. Everything. You can carve anything, carve baroque designs and swirls and flowers. You can carve the human figure. You can carve a horse. There's no limit. The design is mine, or whoever's doing it, and with no restrictions. That's the selfish part of it, I guess.

The altruistic end, we're building something that is going to make it possible for people to appreciate the state. We are, I think, one of the most culturally diverse, if not the richest state, historically, one of the most culturally valuable resources in the country. I want people to appreciate that. I want the kids of New York to understand the cultural heritage that we have. I was appalled to discover that many kids didn't know who Rip Van Winkle was. Kids had not heard of people like Susan B. Anthony. It just seems wrong that these things aren't transmitted from one generation to another, so this is another thing we are trying to do with the carousel. We're trying to revive the art of carousel carving and make that a factor. Not necessarily as a commercial activity, but as just a very joyful and satisfying thing. We're trying to get people involved in the folk arts, and we've succeeded with this to an enormous degree.

I have a very strong thing for the Nineteenth Century. I am artistically a creature of the Nineteenth Century. I guess every artist looks for his essence, his source. Mine is sort of two part. One, it's upstate New York, and secondly, it's the Nineteenth Century. This is what I draw from. So the carousel and upstate New York are coming together very nicely.

I also have a third interest, which is the interest of the immigrant. Primarily, the immigrants who came from Eastern or Southern Europe during the latter part of the Nineteenth Century. This is where most of our carousel carvers came from. I'm Hungarian, Russian, Jewish so I have a relationship with the carvers. Not all of them, but certainly Dentzel and Illions and Lloof. My ancestors came from the same areas which they did, so I have a strong feeling for the immigrants.

I would say the overwhelming majority of the carvers went to work as carvers, carpenters and such, but there were many of them, particularly the chief designers, who saw what they were doing as beautiful works of art. You can't not look at

Figure 91. Master carver Gerry Holzman working on "Percy the Pig" for the Empire State Carousel. (Photo: Courtesy Gerry Holzman)

Figure 92. A completed "Percy" waits among the wood carvers tools for the time he will take his place on the Empire State Carousel. (Photo: Courtesy Gerry Holzman)

some of the Looffs from the 1890s and not see an artist there. I think Gustav Dentzel certainly saw it as a work of art.

The basic concept of the carousel is that it's the animals of New York. One horse. New York's becoming quite a horse breeding state. We have very fine horse racing here. The cow is probably as important to the state as the horse is, so certainly the cow. The beaver is the state symbol. And the squirrels are all over the place. We made up a list of about forty animals that are indigenous to New York state and these are the animals that we've drawn from. We have nine animals that are complete or under construction. Our chariots are a scallop shell and an Erie Canal barge boat.

Our band organ is a very elaborate piece. We commissioned that built by Don Stinson. We designed the facade ourselves, and that organ shows Irving Berlin, John Philip Sousa, George M. Cohan, New York musicians. The facade of it is all New York state fruit and vegetables, corn and grapes and apples and pears, everything from New York.

What's happening is the carousel is just an evolving concept, and it's gotten bigger and bigger. It's not just building a carousel and carving thirty animals. It's frames and moldings and quilts and birds and paintings. We're going to do twenty-four panels on the inside of the rounding boards. We're going to paint the history of the state of New York from twelve hundred up through the modern day with two foot by four foot paintings. That's something we're just getting underway right now.

We figure the total cost of the project somewhere around six hundred thousand dollars. At this point, we've raised about two hundred thousand dollars, and we're about forty percent done. But, I couldn't put a monetary value on it. I couldn't put a monetary value on the group of four women who got together and created a carousel quilting guild. Today, they're one hundred and twenty-five members. It's the most active quilting guild in southern New York. That's not a price.

A guy who has helped to carve the loon, who was about to work on our loon up in the Adirondacks, he died just before the project started. They announced that instead of giving flowers would people give money to the loon fund. The carvers up there used this to buy the wood, and buy the glue, and pay the expenses. Three of them carved the loon. Then they dedicated it to his memory with a brass plaque, and had his grandson take the first ride. Symbolically. We had it on a stand and we put him on the loon. He sat there and posed for pictures and took the symbolic first ride. Those are things that you can't measure in money. They're all part of the carousel.

Art, history, music, and animals are all components of the endless appeal of the merry-go-round. The captivating attraction of the various relationships is nicely summed up in the following comments.

It's different for different people. I think it's different for young people sometimes than it is for older people. For young people, I think it's the fascination with animals in general. My daughter, I know, just has this incredible fascination with animals. All kinds. She just loves animals. Aside from a real animal, a merry-go-round is as close as it gets for many people, for many kids. Kids don't have the opportunity to be around a farm as much as they used to. When you think about it, a merry-go-round horse is the only thing next to a real animal that a person can get on, so I think that would be the appeal to a lot of the kids.

And, I think, a lot of the appeal for adults is just being around the kids and being able to observe the happiness and joy that is evident in a kid's face that's riding a merry-go-round. It's attractive to both young and old.

Scott Bittler

There's a magical mystique about the carousel. You go up there and the horses are so incredibly beautiful, and the colors are so vivid. There's something about little kids always liking vivid colors. A friend of mine said, "Little kids and old people like vivid colors," and so it's the magic of that. The gleam in their eyes. They're so excited when they see it. I still get excited when I go up and see it. The carousel is just one of my favorite things. It's a very special feeling on my part. It's really a family type ride. It appeals to everyone, the young and the old. It's got a special appeal to it.

Randall Bailey

It has a tremendous quality and charm and it's one of the last of its kind to exist.

Joyce Hanks

11

The End of an Era

The "golden years" of the carousel only slightly preceded the "golden era" of amusement parks. Today, both the carousels and the small family-owned parks are disappearing with alarming rapidity. In the 1950s, the theme park concept changed the amusement industry from a small local affair to a corporate business involving millions of dollars. Going to the amusement park was once a local entertainment that children dreamed about and waited for all winter. For a dollar or two a child could spend many happy hours at a park near its home. Today, visiting a theme park more than likely involves the entire family, may require a great deal of travel, and certainly will be an expense the average American family could not afford very often. The merry-go-round itself, once the pride of the midway and an amusement attraction appealing predominantly to the working classes, has evolved into an art object affordable only by the wealthy.

These changes were regretted by all of the participants of the "Carousel Keepers" project, preservationists and collectors alike. The bleak future of the traditional small amusement park and the disappearance of the carousel were strongly felt by everyone and the sadness of these losses was echoed over and over again. Raymond D'Agostino laments the fact that Bertrand Island Amusement Park has ceased to exist.

Figure 93. Aerial view of Bertrand Island Amusement Park, Lake Hopatcong, New Jersey, about 1950. "Bertrand Island is almost in the middle of Lake Hopatcong, and it's gorgeous" — Ray D'Agostino. (Photo: From the collection of Ray D'Agostino)

After Palisades and Olympic closed, Bertrand Island was the only one left. The fellow I sold it to, he operated it for four or five years. Things just weren't going right and he decided to close it up. Really, what happened I don't know. He thought that he could do much better building apartments and town houses than running the amusement park. He is now in the process of getting all of his permits to build town houses and apartments down there. It's a beautiful, beautiful piece of land. All waterfront that I sold him. There's very little lake front left on Lake Hopatcong. It's one of the most beautiful views that you'll ever see. Bertrand Island is almost in the middle of Lake Hopatcong, and it's gorgeous. Bertrand Island Amusement Park was here since 1922. It was started in 1922. I'll tell you, we found out how valuable and how much it was appreciated when they talked about closing it down. People remembered growing up around Lake Hopatcong. Tremendous nostalgia about it. You should see the letters that they were receiving. They say they grew up knowing this amusement park, and what a shame it would be now not to have the amusement park here anymore. And at nighttime, we used to have lights and a lot of the boats used to be able to travel by those lights on the lake. That used to be a point. People would say, "There's Bertrand Island, now we know where we are." We used to have fireworks at nighttime here and people used to be able to sit on their porches and watch it. Now all that stuff is gone.

Of course today you have Disney World and Disney Land. You have these big gigantic parks. They're not the same as these little family-run parks like we had. I'm afraid the day of the small amusement park is gone. It's finished. You just couldn't operate three months of the year and have a profitable or going business. It just can't be done. Years ago, you could operate an amusement park for three months and make a living. You could do that. The insurance, your expenses, your help, everything concerned. It got difficult. And the taxes got so bad. Taxes quadrupled, quintupled, and, my God, they're up and up and up. It's very difficult to try to

Figure 94. Boardwalk at Bertrand Island Amusement Park, Lake Hopatcong, New Jersey, about 1930. "I'm afraid the day of the small amusement park is gone" — Ray D'Agostino. (Photo: From the collection of Ray D'Agostino)

operate three months and make a living. He saw that. You could see it. The trend was there.

Nothing is left. Nothing. They tore it down. Tore it right down. Tore everything down. The gentleman that bought the park from me, he went in and razed everything right down flat to the ground. Because, they figure, when they get all of their permits from the town and county and the state, they want to proceed and start doing things.

I walk by it every morning. I walk by the amusement park, and everyday I remember how I would be hearing the kids hollering, the kids screaming. I used to love to listen. It's just a shame that the children being born today, and the children already here, the small children, will never really appreciate or know what it's like to go to a real hometown amusement park, a family-run amusement park. They will miss all that. They won't see it around this part of Jersey anyway. It's disappearing. It's a shame. That's all dying out now. It's all dying away.

Changing social conditions, waning dress codes, and the decline of traditional values were felt by several interviewees to be factors that contributed to the loss of our traditional parks. Charlotte Dinger bleakly states:

I feel sad about the disappearance of the carousels. You know there's sort of a feeling of collectors having encouraged this, but it's quite the opposite. Collectors really would like to see carousels continue to operate. We love the carousel. But, then on the other hand, some of the animals that we see are so badly neglected and in such terrible condition. Some have legs missing and their bodies have dry rot or the seams are totally separated, which requires the whole animal to be taken completely apart. Parts need to be recarved. There really is an awful lot to it. The maintenance today of a carousel, in order to get it into top condition, can cost four hundred thousand dollars. That's a typical price to restore a complete carousel. And the small park owner simply can't afford that. The carousel doesn't make that kind of money to warrant that sort of a restoration. Another problem that carousel owners are facing is the insurance costs today. Terrible. Of course the brass ring has virtually disappeared because of that. If you have a brass ring mechanism on your carousel, the price of insurance doubles. So you're not seeing many of those in the country anymore. So many people I meet have never been on a carousel with rings. Certainly none of the young people. They don't even know what we're talking about when we say you reach for the brass ring. That's sad because it was a great fun part of the carousel. It's too bad to see that disappear.

And, you know, there's a difference today in attitude. We certainly see it everywhere. And, that is the lack of care about other people's property and even caring about relics of the past. We see evidence of people carving initials in the animals and stepping on the legs to get on the horses instead of on the metal step. Also, I've seen a teenager with one foot on a magnificent lion's head and one foot on the saddle, standing up holding on to the pole.

The family parks are disappearing for a number of reasons. In addition to costs of upkeep, there are rough crowds and vandalism. It's terrible. I saw it happen at Olympic Park. The owner took such wonderful care of his park. There was an enormous swimming pool, but it just got so difficult to keep the park going because kids would climb over the fence for no reason and destroy so many of the rides and the booths. Even throwing glass into the pool. I hear this from all over the country. It isn't that dealers are putting pressure on owners to sell their carousels. There are many reasons why these parks are breaking up. One reason in the last ten years that has caused the demise of many parks is their prime locations on lakes and beaches which attracts land developers.

There were a lot more carousels than there are today. In the back of my book, I have a census of the parks that were

Figure 95. The copper roof, graceful cupola, and stained glass windows make the Casino Building in Asbury Park, New Jersey, a wonderful example of symmetrical elegance in carousel architechture. (Photo: Carrie Papa)

here in 1983 when I wrote the book. A number of those have disappeared.

The carousel that bothered me probably more than any in New Jersey that disappeared is the one on the Asbury Park boardwalk in a wonderful building. It is in the finest carousel building that I have ever seen, the greatest building in the country. Just marvelous. I've never seen one that is as nice anywhere.

Asbury Park was a wonderful place. I remember going to Asbury Park as a child. I remember it in its glory days when it was a great vacation place. There was the water ride, and the swan ride and the Ferris wheel that went out through the top of a building and overlooked the water. I remember all that.

The Asbury Park that Charlotte remembers so fondly has changed considerably. Palace Amusements was sold to make room for beach-front redevelopment. Bill Foster, manager of Palace before the sale, explains the owner's difficulties in trying to retain the wonderful four-abreast Loofe carousel and to keep the Palace operating.

We had a Senator, or I guess a Congressman, who was helping out and he tried to get funds, state funds and federal funds to save the carousel and the horses and that was unsuccessful. Initially, we weren't going to sell it. The intentions of the owner was to take that carousel and put it in a new location. See, with the redevelopment of the city, everyone knew that the Palace was earmarked to go eventually, within two years, three years, five years. It was really uncertain, so we tried to maintain the business as best we could. We spent a lot of money to restore the carousel and keep it. We put one hundred thousand dollars into the carousel. We put another quarter of a million into new machinery, new rides, to try and boost our business. To try to keep going.

Well, that summer we had that ocean pollution problem and business dropped to approximately fifty-five percent. So, we got together and we decided, "Hey, we're knocking our heads against the wall trying to make this business flow and it's not doing it." We wound up losing hundreds of thousands of dollars every year. We never gained back what we had put into it, plus normal costs exceeded our revenue. So, after the pollution problem, we said, "That's it. Let's just close early and get out before we lose too much."

I have an old sketch that was in a 1934 newspaper advertising the Palace and the carousel. The Palace was a family-owned business. At one time, they had the Palace, the Casino, all along the boardwalk, all the rides. They had the motor boats and the swans in the lake and the paddle boats. It was really the place to go.

Things run in cycles. In the thirties and forties and part of the fifties, you had people with a lot of enthusiasm towards the carousel. During the late fifties, sixties, seventies, people got away from that. They got into the "ME" generation and really put no value on anything. Parks started to disband because of the economics in the past twenty years. You didn't have the large parks. You didn't have the Great Adventures. You didn't have Action Parks. All you had were the tiny, Mom and Pop amusement parks and that's where people went. Where people went for enjoyment was the local amusement park. Well, now you have better transportation. Everybody has automobiles. The highway system is a lot faster now. It's nothing for anybody these days to drive down to Busch Gardens, Virginia, for a weekend and drive back. They're not going to the little place.

Another cycle that's changed is that both parents are working now. They both can't get their vacations at the same time. Used to be twenty years ago, people came down to the shore and they spent a whole week or a month or the whole summer down here. The husband would commute back to New York. And this would go on anywhere around the country that way.

This is why there's such a problem in the United States now for the small amusement park, and the carousels being broken up. The small amusement parks cannot afford them. Business is slow. Insurance costs are sky rocketing. Labor costs are going up, and they can't afford to operate.

The only way to save their park and save their business is when you have a carousel that's sitting there and it's worth a million dollars. You can take a million dollars worth of horses or seven hundred thousand dollars worth of horses and for one hundred thousand dollars or less, depending on the size of the carousel, you can re-outfit it with fiber-glass horses and have a half a million dollars left over to keep your business going. So that's really what's happening.

You don't have people coming into Asbury Park like they used to. The new development has made it worse. They started tearing all the buildings down. They cut off Ocean Avenue. So, people coming into town, it looks like a bombed area.

We tried to keep the carousel. There was nothing more we could do to keep it together. We tried to do the best we could, but it's a business too, and you can't just say, "Well, I'm going to throw a half a million dollars out the window so I can preserve the carousel."

Edward Lange, the former owner of the Palace Amusements who spent his life in Asbury Park, also comments on the changes that took place during the past twenty years.

We operated for forty-eight years. I hate to even go to Asbury Park now. That was my life over there. When I came to Asbury Park, it was a prime resort. First there was Atlantic City, number one, and Asbury Park, number two. I'm talking about fifty, sixty years ago. It's an era that's gone. For so many years it was fine. The people were nice. They were dressed very properly. In later years, kinda ragamuffins. They come in T-shirts and sweat shirts. They became so different. People were well dressed in those days. Dressed quite decently. Just so different. And towards the end it became very ragtag. Not at all the way it used to be in the beginning.

The decline started in 1970, when we had the racial riots. You remember when Newark and Detroit and Los Angeles had all these racial riots. Well, we had it in 1970 and from there on, it started sliding. Little by little business went from bad to worse. The clientele became lesser quality. More of the rough elements came in. Many parks had problems. Some parks closed up. When the people were better dressed, they were better mannered also. There was much less dirt. People put things in receptacles. Now they go and put it on the floor.

The nicer people stopped coming, little by little. The clientele became lesser quality. From 1970, well, it didn't go down radically, just a slow sag. Asbury Park went down the drain. Complete disaster. Asbury Park is in very bad shape. It's down in the dumps. There's only half a dozen concessionaires on the boardwalk. It's completely dead. No people. Asbury Park is dead. It's an era that's gone.

Figure 96. In the 1950's, one wore a suit and tie when taking a date to Palisades Amusement Park. (Photo: Courtesy Richard Scheiss)

Terry Cicalese is yet another respondent who laments the loss of the merry-go-rounds and the changes at the New Jersey shore.

> Point Pleasant Beach had a beautiful, large merry-go-round. It was in a building off the boardwalk. When you rode the merry-go-round, you would try to catch the brass ring for an extra ride. Even before the children were born, when I was going out with my husband, we rode the merry-go-round. That's when everybody got dressed up to come on to the boardwalk. You had to wear a shirt. You couldn't walk in a bathing suit without a cover up.
>
> The dress code is completely changed. Like anyplace else, I guess. Now you can wear what you want and your bathing suit doesn't have to be covered. You can wear the skimpiest bathing suit. I see changes, but I think it's the changes in people more than changes in the town. It's so hard to say. People just don't take care of things the way they did years ago. When they use things, it just isn't the way it used to be.
>
> I guess maybe they don't consider riding a merry-go-round as much fun as we did when we were younger. We enjoyed riding the merry-go-round and taking a walk on the boardwalk. That's when they used to have the homemade taffy. They would make it right on the boardwalk. They don't do that anymore either.
>
> The only rides that are still left here are the children's rides. Little children. That carousel burned in a fire. The horses were beautiful, but at that time, it was a carousel for riding and nobody thought about it. There is no merry-go-round now. It's changed.

The demise of Eldridge Park in Elmira, New York, is explained in Scott Bittler's recollection.

> Eldridge Park suffered from a lot of things that are common to the problems that a lot of small family parks across America suffer from. That is, that there's a number of things in society that compete for entertainment time that people have to spend that didn't exist back in the old days. You know, a trip to the park on a weekend was one of the few things you could do for entertainment outside of your home back in the old days. But today, there's the existence of large

theme parks. Competitiveness in the entertainment arena, it suffered from that.

I think the fact that the community began to take it for granted as something that was just there and would be there all the time, it was that. It was also the fact that my grandparents were aging. They were in their seventies and my grandfather was failing in health. One of the major problems with the park that ultimately led to its demise was the lease arrangement with the city.

Unlike most parks which are entirely a private enterprise, Eldridge Park was largely unique in that the property is owned by the City of Elmira. Donated by the late Edwin Eldridge many, many years ago, and this was done with the intent of it being used as a park. The involvement of my family in the park was by lease of the land from the city. They had sub-lease concessionaires that had various interests in the park concessions as well. But my grandfather and my father were the primaries and were the owners of all the rides, for example. There was a constant bickering over what responsibilities the city had for upkeep of the property and the picnic grounds, for example, and what was the responsibility of the lease holder. This was a constant battle that prevented a lot of development of the facilities that might have occurred.

It suffered from that. The aging of the equipment in some of these old parks and the increasing maintenance costs on that. The roller coaster, for example, we spent incredible sums to keep it up. Insurance costs rising is a big problem that creates an economic difficulty. You see many family parks suffering from the same kinds of pressures.

When the park was sold, I think, it suffered from the fact that the person that became involved in the park at that time just didn't have amusement business experience. What happened was, when we sold the park, we didn't have it in our hearts to sell the merry-go-round because it was the focal point of our whole family's involvement. We wanted to do everything we could for as long as we could to keep it, number one, together as a complete operating unit, and number two, in operation preferably there at Eldridge Park where it had been for so many years. In fact, during these last years, my immediate family, as owners of the carousel, were subleasing the merry-go-round building facilities. We continued to try to do that for as long as we could financially.

Finally, it did go to auction in New York City a year ago [1990] this past December. Although it was offered as an entire unit at the end of the auction, there was no one to bid, so it did go to individuals. It saddens me because it's a piece of Americana that future generations just won't know of. It holds a lot of fond memories from my own upbringing that we won't be able to share with our kids.

The change in the kind of people coming to the seashore and riding the merry-go-round is once again described by Dell Hopson, another long time carousel manager at the Jersey shore.

We built a summer home in Seaside Heights in 1914. I was on the boardwalk and around the merry-go-round all the time. I'm talking about my childhood now. I fed the rings to the customers on the merry-go-round. The brass ring. That kind of thing during my growing-up period. It was a very beautiful merry-go-round. We try to keep it running in good operation. And, you know, a lot of people, especially younger people, they don't really appreciate what it's worth and what it represents. So they're not too careful with the way they act with it. So, it is a problem of disciplining and supervising them so that they don't tear it down around your ears.

Seaside Heights was settled primarily by Philadelphians. After awhile, the people who came to Seaside Heights came from Trenton and that area. After that, they came from North Jersey. Now they're coming from Long Island and New York. The people that first came down here were very nice people. They were family people. A good many of them came down here as a summer home. They were here practically the whole summer when the schools were closed. And when you walked down the street, you knew practically everybody that lived in town. Then, it gradually changed to where we got excursion people.

When the Garden State Parkway opened, it started to slowly change to day trippers. They come in by automobile because the train's no longer run down here. I feel bad about saying this, but the clientele that came down seems to have deteriorated in makeup as against the people who originally were here and who were renters at one time. A lot of them are just kids down here to raise all kinds of devilment. It's an entirely different town than what it was when I grew up.

As those types of people infiltrated into our economy, they were the ones that were tougher on the merry-go-round operation. It's a lack of concern not only for the merry-go-round, but everything that's in the town. I'm sorry to say that the clientele that comes to Seaside Heights now — and I hate to advertise this, but you asked me to tell you — has deteriorated. I plant flowers out in my front yard. They pull the flowers out and throw them in the street. They throw beer bottles and beer cans all over my front yard. Sometimes, I get a whole trash can full of trash in the morning after a weekend or after Saturday night. And that never used to be. I think a lot of the towns along the Jersey coast have suffered this same kind of an influx. Unfortunately. It has to change. It cannot remain that way or all the good people will start staying away. We don't want the good people to stay away. We want them to come down.

The town grew, and as it grew, it changed character slowly. The change was sometimes so slow, you hardly even noticed it. It's changed.

Like so many small traditional parks, Palisades Amusement Park in Cliffside, New Jersey, closed in 1970. However, as Sol Abrams makes plain, Palisades closed not because it suffered from the many problems plaguing other local parks, but for entirely different reasons.

Other parks were larger. We only had thirty-eight acres. Nobody, nobody would dream that there was only thirty-eight acres. But we had attendance! And that was one of the reasons for the demise of the park. When the park was built, it was built at the end of the trolley line as most of the early parks were. People didn't have cars then. Parks originally were a way to get revenue for the transit company. That's who built the park originally. It was called the Bergen Traction Company, which eventually became Public Service of New Jersey, and today, it's called New Jersey Transport.

To give you an idea of the type of audience we had, the last year that the park was open, we got a call in advance

Figure 97. This winter scene just before the demolition of Palisades Amusement Park seems to symbolize the depressing final days of the once great amusement center. (Photo: Newark Public Library)

Figure 98. Sol Abrams and the luxury Winston Towers, which were built on the site of Palisades Amusement Park, Cliffside Park, New Jersey. (Photo: Courtesy Sol Abrams)

and a van came up with Jackie Onassis, John-John and Carolyn and their friends. The park was open and they just came in. They just didn't want people to flood around them so they kept a little circle of security around. So we were getting the crowds, but we didn't have parking. They bought parking area along the Hudson and Edgewater and bussed people up. We couldn't accommodate the crowds. It was *TOO* successful. Every year the attendance went up over the year before. But there was no parking space left for the increasing number of motorists who came to the park. Our crowds and traffic grew and our parking areas diminished.

A few years ago, I was asked to pose for a picture atop the Palisades, close by the original site. It tore my heart out. As I stood here in the rubble of the park, where they were ready to build the luxury Winston Towers, I looked down. I started to cry. I was standing near the spot where the merry-go-round used to be.

It is tragic that so many fun centers have not been able to make a go of it in recent years. Countless children are being deprived of the fun and excitement that their older brothers, sisters, and parents experienced at Palisades Amusement Park. We even kept a hole in the fence on purpose so that no kid should be denied getting into the park. It was a labor of love. I miss it.

Richard Scheiss provides another view of Palisades Amusement Park and the changes over the past few years.

We had a regular class of people. Not high class. Regular class. You go to the park, you know you're going to spend a few dollars. It was cheap to get in. Thirty-five cents to get in. If you had a park pass, it cost you a dime. Now you don't see that. To get into a park now it cost you about twenty-two dollars or twenty-three dollars to get into Great Adventure. Theme parks now are more expensive than the park they had here. You could bring your own lunch if you wanted. People used to do that. Bring their lunch and have a picnic. Then go on the rides. Things gradually changed. Went up. Tuesdays and Thursdays at that time were "Bargain Days." The rides were five and ten cents. After six o'clock, they were ten cents. The busiest days were Tuesdays and Thursdays, because of "Bargain Days." Maybe seven thousand or more people on those days.

The park was great for everybody. It helped the kids and everything to keep out of trouble. That's how I look at it. It was the main thing for everybody. If that park was still there, these kids today would be having jobs for the summer to keep them out of trouble. They would have money coming. Money in their pocket. Now there's nothing. The kids hang around and do nothing all summer. Drugs are all over.

At that time, there was nothing. No marijuana. Nothing. It's a big difference. It's a big change. Very big change. I wish things would go back. That place really brought back the memories for a lot of people. We had such good times in that park. We always had parties and stuff. Whose having a party here, whose having a party there.

They have a place, a restaurant up here called Memories. It's been there a couple years now and they have a lot of stuff from the park. Memories, in Fort Lee. We get together there and talk about the old times. We look at the video of Palisades and we could cry.

Unfortunately, memories are all that many of us have left of the golden era of the local amusement park. As with a number of special carousels, many of our favorite parks simply are no more.

How is your Memory of Amusement Parks Past?

(Match the Park with the City of these Parks Sold by Norton)

Buck Lake Ranch	Custer, SD
Petticoat Junction	Geneseo, NY
Idora Park	Franklinton, NC
Encanto Kiddieland	Middletown, OH
Crystal Beach	Altoona, PA
Volmars Park	Youngstown, OH
Long Point Park	Cherokee, NC
Roseland	Rochester, NY
Beech Bend Park	Zanesville, OH
Arkland	Panama City Beach, FL
Enchanted Forest	Paducah, KY
Boyertown	Phoenix, AZ
Wild West World	Saratoga Springs, NY
Fantasy Farm	Canandaiqua Lake, NY
Magic Waters	Detroit, MI
Joyland Park	Angola, IN
Olympic Park	Ontario, Canada
Moxahalla Park	Moosic, PA
Twin Lakes Park	Bowling Green, KY
Nobles Park Funland	Bowling Green, OH
Hanson's Park	Porter, IN
Kaydeross Park	Alexandria, LA
White Swan Park	Nantasket Beach, MA
Edgewater	Lemont, IL
Pine Lake Park	Topeka, KS
City Park Funland	Ocean City, NJ
Angela Park	Hudson, NH
Fair Park	New London, CT
Rocky Glen	Paris, IL
Dispensa's Kiddie Kingdom	Harveys Lake, PA
Acorn Ridge	Coloma, MI
Gillian's Fun Deck	Pittsburgh, PA
Bensons	Caroga Lake, NY
Ocean Beach Park	Nashville, TN
Paragon	Oak Brook Terrace, IL
Fun Fair	Hazelton, PA
Deer Forest	Point Pleasant Beach, NJ
Lakeview	Royersford, PA

Figure 99. Do you remember where any of these amusement parks were located? See answers on following page. (Courtesy Daniel Satow, Norton Auctioneers)

Answers
The parks matched with their proper cities

ACORN RIDGE	LEMONT, IL
ANGELA PARK	HAZELTOWN, PA
ARKLAND	FRANKLINTON, NC
BEECH BEND PARK	BOWLING GREEN, KY
BENSONS	HUDSON, NH
BOYERTOWN	ALTOONA, PA
BUCK LAKE RANCH	ANGOLA, IN
CITY PARK FUNLAND	ALEXANDRIA, LA
CRYSTAL BEACH	ONTARIO CANADA
DEER FOREST	COLOMA, MI
DISPENSA'S KIDDIELAND	CHICAGO, IL
EDGEWATER	DETROIT, MI
ENCANTO KIDDIELAND	PHOENIX, AZ
ENCHANTED FOREST	PORTER, IN
FAIR PARK	NASHVILLE, TN
FANTASY FARM	MIDDLETOWN, OH
FUN FAIR PARK	POINT PLEASANT BCH, NJ
GILLIANS FUN DECK	OCEAN CITY, NJ
HANSONS PARK	HARVEY'S LAKE, PA
IDORA PARK	YOUNGSTOWN, OH
JOYLAND PARK	TOPEKA, KS
KAYDEROSS PARK	SARATOGA SPGS, NY
LAKEVIEW PARK	ROYERSFORD, PA
LONG POINT PARK	GENESEO, NY
MAGIC WATERS	CHEROKEE, NC
MAXAHALLA PARK	ZANESVILLE, OH
NOBLES PARK FUNLAND	PADUCAH, KY
OCEAN BCH PARK	NEW LONDON, CT
OLYMPIC PARK	ROCHESTER, NY
PARAGON PARK	NANTASKET BCH, MA
PETTICOAT JUNCTION	PANAMA CITY BCH, FL
PINE LAKE PARK	CAROGA, NY
ROCKY GLEN PARK	MOOSIC, PA
ROSELAND	CANANDAIGUA LAKE, NY
TWIN LAKES PARK	PARIS. IL
VOLLMERS PARK	BOWLING GREEN, OH
WHITE SWAN PARK	PITTSBURGH, PA
WILD WEST WORLD	CUSTER, SD

12

To Bring Joy to People

No one can predict what will be the future of America's few remaining old-fashioned parks and antique carousels. In a few years will there be any family-owned, local parks left? At the end of the century, will the only place to see a carousel figure be in a museum? We don't know. We can only hope that some traditional parks will survive and that some vintage carousels will continue operating.

If we can judge from plans some of the narrators have for the future, tomorrow may not be as bleak as was once forecast. A sign that we can hope for the best is found in the emphatic statement of Al Reid, co-owner of Keansburg Amusement Park.

> We are an attraction in that you can see something different here than a regular stamped out theme park someplace. This is different here. We've got personality. I always say we're pregnant with personality. We make french fries like they did back fifty years ago. We make different stuff here. Everything is individual.
>
> I do like busmen's holidays. I will go to the amusement areas, but I'm much more excited if I can find a place like this rather than trying Busch Gardens or Knotts Farm or Great Adventure because they are a stamp-out plastic thing. There's a plastic personality on all of them, I don't care what you say. I like to go to a place where they haven't centrally planned it in some board room. It's getting more and more difficult to find that kind of place today.

Figure 100. Nestled amid an oak grove in Recreation Park, Binghamton, New York, the Allan Herschell carousel was donated by Lillian Sweet, the daughter of George F. Johnson, and installed in 1925. The pavilion is sixteen-sided with a cupola and flagpole. Because of their uniqueness and the special circumstances of their existence, all six Broome County carousels are listed on the National Register of Historic Sites. (Photo: Ed Aswad, Carriage House Photography)

I get great satisfaction out of meeting a customer's need, making money doing it and seeing somebody happy. I don't think there's a better combination in the world. I think that's what should motivate business people, because it makes you happy. Money is how you keep score perhaps, but [what you do] is what makes you happy.

You asked if Keansburg is going to go out of business. No! No, it's not. It's not so. It may never go out of business. And that's something, I'd like to make clear. I hope you quote me on that.

In Ocean City, New Jersey, another amusement pier owner, Roy Gillian, echoes similar sentiments. The town is thriving and business is good.

We're considered, I think, the sixteenth richest community in the state of New Jersey. Out of five hundred sixty-seven. We are a tourist area. We go from a twenty thousand winter population up to about one-hundred-twenty-five or one-hundred-fifty during a weekend in the summer. We just have a super nice class of people that come here and the people that live here year round. We have very little rowdyism. We are so fortunate in this town. Of all the years, I've been here, I've never had a night watchman. I've never had any real problems, real vandalism.

With my business here, I've always tried to run it and keep it up to date and make it look presentable. I'm proud of it. In the summertime when people walk around here, they see it's well cared for. I've just had one of the best years I've ever had. The fact is, I have to admit, that over the past twenty-five years, I've increased my income every year except one. It was just one of those years. But every other year, I've increased my base.

This past year [1989] I bought four new rides. The big wheel was used. If you buy a big wheel like that, you can put almost a million dollars in it. I had probably a little over two hundred thousand dollars in this one by the time I bought it. It cost me fifty grand to move it up here. I bought one other major ride, that balloon ride out there, that was two-hundred-fifteen thousand dollars. The little kid ride was forty-five thousand dollars so they are expensive. A coaster this size now you couldn't get for less than a million. The one they put up in Great Adventure, I think they put six or seven million in that new coaster. It's definitely become big business. The big wheel, which you can see from the Parkway now, draws people. They don't have to drive all the way down to Wildwood. I know that the merchants along the boardwalk are very thankful that we're here.

The city now is just undertaking establishing a historic district, tie in the business section with the boardwalk and some of these nice old houses in the center of the town. Just kind of create an atmosphere that the people could enjoy walking around.

I see people walk by and they'll stop and they'll look at the merry-go-round. They'll just stand there and admire it. A lot of them will take pictures of it. It's always the backbone of the amusement park. I don't think I've ever been in any of them that never had one of some sort. It seems like there's always a merry-go-round in the center of the park someplace. It's one of the staple rides, and I'll tell you, it's a high grosser. It does well. It rides many many people every night. This is a #75, serial number, Philadelphia Toboggan, and it was built somewhere around 1920–1922.

I see these auctions that come around and I know the value of those eighteen outside horses. I know I've got something that's worth something there. I've been told that I should take all those outside horses off and just put them in storage and that would take care of my retirement. [laughter] But, I haven't been in that dire need of finances. I always say that if I ever got to the point of having to do that, then I would really be in big trouble. But, I have never considered doing that. I'm proud of it. I look at it as one of the major attractions of the pier. It's right out there in the front. Most of the people that come in, it's the first thing that they see. I try to take care of it and make it look good. We shine the brass every day, and keep it clean, mopped. It's part of our business. We're proud of it.

Figure 101. Four generations of Gillians — David Gillian and grandsons, Stephen, Jim and Jay, son Roy and great grandson Ryan. The Gillians have been involved with the amusement industry in Ocean City, New Jersey, since 1929. It is anticipated that baby Ryan will continue the family tradition. (Photo: Courtesy Roy Gillian)

As recently as 1987, there were twenty-one operating historic carousels in New Jersey. Today, there are only three left that are open to the public. Fortunately these seem to be quite safe. As we've just read, Roy Gillian in Ocean City does not consider selling his classic Philadelphia Toboggan Company merry-go-round. Robert Bennett, the other private owner of an amusement pier and vintage carousel in New Jersey, also confirmed that he has no intention of letting his carousel go to auction or any other place.

I don't ever want to retire. I love the business. I live in Seaside Park. I refuse to live more than five or ten minutes from my job, because I want to be here. If it's eight in the morning till two in the morning, it doesn't make any difference. In the summer months, I have to be here day and night, day and night. Off season, it's kinda a nine to five job. In the wintertime, everything comes off the pier. It all goes into the shop. Get's painted, repairing this, replacing this. Now it's just starting to come back out. They're setting things up now. I had two new rides come in from Italy yesterday, two new kiddie rides that are going in there. This section right in the center here, they're all kiddie rides. Then this whole other section, out around the top is all major rides. We cater to the family. We don't say we're for just teenagers, or just kids. We're trying to create something for the whole family.

The carousel, that's the family ride. The mother, the father and the kids will get on the merry-go-round. The merry-go-round seems to satisfy everyone. I don't have any carousel horses in my home. In fact, you know there are so many people that get mad at people for breaking up carousel horses and selling them off as individual pieces to people that want to put them in their houses. So, I've just always kinda felt a little reluctant to be part of that. In other words, if I'm in the carousel business, I'm not part of the people that are breaking them up, so I decided that I didn't want one in my house.

Of course, when you see somebody that doesn't respect what they're doing. When they go to get on the horse, when they step on the leg of the horse or something like that to try to boost themselves up on it, or do something they're not supposed to be doing, it makes you feel bad. But hopefully, there's enough people out there that will appreciate it or do appreciate it that that's the way we'll continue. It's a big part of the attraction. We constantly, constantly advertise it.

The other end of the pier had a wood carousel. They sold that. This year that went and they're replacing that with a fiberglass. Probably, if we took ours and replaced it with a fiberglass one, probably dollars and cents wise, we'd take in the same amount of money. But, I just feel there's a certain amount of pride that goes with owning an antique carousel. A real one, not a fiberglass one. And I'm happy to say that I own one. And that we have the original organ on there that plays all the original rolled music like it was back in the early 1900s. Like, I said, I really don't have any intention at all of ever selling it.

Floyd [Moreland] asked me about it one day — I guess he got nervous when he heard what they're getting for these. I said to him, "Floyd, as long as you're here, don't ever worry about that carousel going anyplace." He worries about every light bulb and every tail on every horse and everything. As long as there's someone like him there to worry about it, then I wouldn't think of selling it.

Figure 102. Floyd L. Moreland with his favorite horse, "Dr. Floyd," on the historic Dentzel/Looff carousel, Seaside Heights, New Jersey. (Photo: Dr. Norma B. Menghetti)

The third classic carousel in New Jersey belongs to Six Flags Great Adventure. The time may come when only the large theme parks have the finances and the resources to maintain and protect historic carousels. Certainly many of the merry-go-rounds that have been sold or auctioned as complete units have gone to the corporate parks. Ultimately, the great theme parks may become the last keepers of the carousels. The Six Flags Corporation has a vintage carousel in each of their parks. William Moore, former General Manager of Six Flags Great Adventure in Jackson, New Jersey, explained the importance of their carousel to the park.

> Our carousel was built by Mr. Savage in England. The carousel was originally steam driven. The state ride inspectors would not allow the carousel to operate as a steam driven ride. They felt that was unsafe. So, they had an engineer come in and he simply changed the method of operations to compressed air. It operates that way today. So, the actual drive mechanism is still intact as it originally was, but it's driven by compressed air.

Figure 103. The Victorian look of the carousel pavilion at Six Flags Great Adventure, Jackson, New Jersey, was part of the original design of the park. The Savage Gallopers carousel, built in England sometime between 1881 and 1890, was the focus point for the original park. (Photo: Six Flags Theme Parks)

In Great Adventure's history, it's taken a very prominent place. The only other change, major change, the ride originally came here with a canvas roof on it. We've since built a wood roof over the top of the ride that is a little more serviceable and gives the carousel a lot more protection.

During the wintertime, we take care to redo the horses, touch them up or repaint them, fix any broken parts. We pride ourselves on maintenance. Any kind of major maintenance, we do it when it's needed, even if it's during the summer. If it's needed, we just stop and do it. We have talked a little bit about redoing the way the mechanisms work mechanically to make it a little bit more modern. It uses some beveled gears out on the ends to drive the shafts and whatnot. Those, in today's time, are not the best method to make the horses jump and all that, but it's something we just have chosen not to do. Even though there are better ways to do it, you kind of hate to mess with the carousel.

Our company has a history of restoring carousels. We just restored one at Six Flags Over Texas. The carousel that I'm really closest too is the carousel at Six Flags Over Georgia, which is a Philadelphia Toboggan unit. I believe it was constructed around 1905 and actually resided in the Chicago area for a long time. I know we've been able to verify that Al Capone rode it and some of the more notorious gangsters. We bought the ride in the early seventies and shipped it to Georgia. It was in very, very poor condition years ago. It was completely restored and sits there today on top of a hill.

We've [the Six Flags Corporation] never sold a carousel or gotten rid of one. They are a major part of the original design. Most of the other rides, you could go buy another one. The wooden coaster, I guess, is probably the only other ride that we have that you just can't replace. We toyed around a little bit with the columns that go around the outside of the building. We've repainted the color of those two or three different times. Last year, we had it a real modern art deco kind of look, and all of us hated it. It was almost — gosh, I almost want to say purple — but, I guess, it was a plum kind of color on the outside. We all yelled about it, all year long. We didn't think it was proper for a carousel to have that kind of look. Very modern looking. So this winter, we changed it all

228

and went back to a very traditional candy cane look around there.

Our plans are to keep all the horses as they are as long as we possibly can. In Six Flags, all of our parks have carousels and nobody wants to take them out or have them sold. It would be a shame one day if little kids didn't have any carousels to ride. As long as we're here, that carousel is going to stay right there and be maintained.

Six Flags Over Georgia saved the 1908 Philadelphia Toboggan Company carousel originally manufactured for the grand opening of Chicago's Riverview Park. After Riverview Park was razed in 1966 to make way for a new housing development, the seventy intricately carved horses were stored and nearly forgotten until Six Flags Over Georgia rescued the magnificent

Figure 104. PTC #17 was built in 1903, specifically for the grand opening of Chicago's Riverview Park. It was housed in a beautiful Victorian Pavilion, which was demolished in 1966. (Photo: From the collection of the National Amusement Park Historical Association)

merry-go-round from oblivion. The five-abreast carousel is one of only three such machines remaining in the world. In January 1995, "for its significance in the history of American recreation and engineering, and as an outstanding example of the work of master woodcarver Leo Zoller," the carousel was listed on the National Register of Historic Places.

In addition to Al Capone, this carousel's famous riders included William Randolph Hearst and President Warren G. Harding, as well as a more recent president. Randall Bailey and Kim Fraker are very proud that Six Flags Over Georgia has this particular carousel.

> The park philosophy that we have is that in theming the park they always looked for original things to go along with the theming of the park that would add to the ambiance, rather than something new and modern. I was here when we put it together, the chariots and horses restoration and stuff like that.

> At the time, our General Manager was Errol McCoy — we were of course a historical theme park — and he was really big on keeping history a part of our themed area. He wanted a spectacular carousel, the most spectacular there was that he could find in the country. He had heard about the one at Riverview Park. He knew it was in existence when he started his search. He found it in a warehouse in a little town in Illinois. The town had purchased it and they decided they didn't want to repair it or whatever. Six Flags made an offer on it.

> It was in pretty bad disrepair. We moved it down here. They started the process of restoration. It was a five-abreast. We knew that there was not a five-abreast in operation at the time so we were real excited about that. The other thing that he wanted to do was to make it historically, with everything that's possible, as close to the setting as it was at Riverview Park. That was quite a park, in the amusement park industry's eyes looking back on old parks. They had little innovative rides and innovative things.

> He wanted the carousel building to be as close to the Riverview one as possible. When you go out and see the design, you'll see a picture of the one at Riverview, and you see the actual area, it's much like the one was at Riverview. We wanted to keep it that way.

Figure 105. PTC #17 is the last five abreast carousel in operation today. When Riverview Park closed, the magnificent carousel was rescued, restored, and installed in 1972 by Six Flags Over Georgia in an elegant pavilion modeled after the original. (Photo: Six Flags Theme Parks)

The other thing we wanted to do was make sure that we kept it in an area where there was nothing else. It was all by itself. And we just kept it that way until last year. We moved our little antique car ride. They're turn of the century cars and it really themed in nice. With the adding of the Georgia Cyclone, we needed to move those cars. So we moved them to go around it. So, it's really kinda neat because you've got the turn-of-the-century cars going around the bottom of the hill with the carousel on top of the hill. It's kind of a sacred area to us up there.

There's a plaque out front explaining the history of the carousel. It's got a picture of the original building so they can get an idea of what the original building looked like. The only thing we haven't added yet — as I say, Al Capone rode it and President Harding rode it — we didn't add that President Carter rode it so we need to add that eventually.

While he was Governor of the state of Georgia, his family came out every year. They always made at least one trip out. And when he was President, and when he would go to Plains — the four years that he was President, he always came to the park. The Secret Service would usually call us the day

231

before saying that President Carter and his family would like to come to spend the day at the park. They would come out and bring the grand kids. A lot of times they would just bring the grand kids — just to go to the Kiddie Land rides and go to the carousel and go home, depending on the day, and depending on how busy and how hot it was and the temperament of the grand kids. People would recognize them. He would always go over and shake hands, and Roslyn and the whole family would. They were very congenial.

We're extremely proud of the carousel. The guys and girls that work up there, we try to give them an overview of the history of the carousel and a good working knowledge of it. Because Riverview Park was such an incredible park for so many years and there are so many Chicago transplants in Atlanta, and they find out that that was in Riverview, and they'll say, "Oh, I rode this when I was a little kid, you know. In Chicago. I can't believe it." Then they'll go on and on and on about what a beautiful job we did.

Another thing we did, we have rocking chairs around. Instead of just traditional park benches sitting around, we have rocking chairs. That's something we try to keep 'cause the families, the Grandmas, like to sit and rock in the rocking chairs while the little ones ride. We try to give it a real family atmosphere.

Between nine hundred thousand and a million people ride it every year. It's incredible that that's lasted since the early 1900s. The whole thing is incredible, to go in and see the old original carvings on the mast. There's an old ship's mast on the inside, the center pole. Maintenance is continual. Every day. Every day, Art and Sign, go check the carousel every single day to make sure there's no nicks in the horses or anything. Art and Sign take care of the painting of the horses. They have a sealed coating on them, which really does help to preserve the wood from deterioration. The last time it was restored, repainted, stripped down and everything, we made sure that it was sealed real good.

Last year we had a leg break. If something happens like a leg breaks, they immediately take the horse off and take it to the shop and start work on it. It's checked by Art and Sign. It's checked by mechanics. It's checked by the electricians every day. And we have a safety check that we run through every day as well so it's thoroughly checked. Everybody watches over the carousel.

It's very sad that so many carousels have disappeared. Having been in the amusement park industry, it's like one of those things, you want to run out and buy them and save them. I see that as the amusement park industry's whole goal, making people happy. As I said, when you walk out in that park and you see little kids and they're just jumping for joy and they have this special little gleam in their eye about the magic of coming to Six Flags, the magic of riding the carousel, it's very special.

Figure 106. Carved by Leo Zoller, the sixty-nine horses on PTC #17 are among the finest in the world. (Photo: Six Flags Theme Parks)

Last year, I went to San Francisco and a gentleman at the rent a car counter said, "You're from Georgia?" And then, he asked where I worked, and I said, "Six Flags," and he said, "That was my most memorable vacation my family ever took. "We went back East," he said, "My mother was from Georgia. We went to Six Flags," he said, "I'll never forget the carousel." He said, "In my childhood memories, that was. . . ." "Oh," he said, "That is the most. . . . that is the . . . ." Oh, he got so excited. You could see the little kid come back out of him again remembering what a good time he had. So, it makes me feel good that we do a wonderful thing and we have a great job in that we make people happy.

Other carousels, that are fairly secure and unlikely to go to the auctioneer's block are those owned by non-profit organizations such as Washington Cathedral's All Hallows Guild and Martha's Vineyard Preservation Trust. All Hallows Guild is considering a resolution or some other long range plan to protect their carousel in the future. Jane Lee, the person most responsible for All Hallows Guild owning a merry-go-round, feels certain that the carousel is safe.

There will always be people who don't care, but there will always be people who do. We're saving it for the people who do care about an original. There are a lot of people who appreciate what we're hanging on to. It's just the difference in a Matisse and a reproduction of a Matisse. I mean, we've got the real McCoy.

Two years ago, the artist's association [The National Association of Tole and Decorative Painters] were hosts to the national organization, their annual convention, right here in Washington. At least three thousand people came to that. Their logo was the carousel horse Gigi that they had painted. There's a story, it's been republished now and there's a dedication in the forward about Gigi finding a new home at Washington National Cathedral. It's a happy story. Again, that created so much more interest all through the country about an antique carousel because that was their logo for the national convention. This group adopted us — they are charged to do a community project every year — so, as of eight years ago, they adopted us as their community project.

Without their help, we could not go into the expense of total restoration. The National Association of Tole and Decorative Painters, folk art is very popular now, and this is their main talent. Rosemaling and that sort of thing, which is just perfect for our horses. And this is just almost an undiscovered field up until recently. It's the pebble in the pond and all the ripples. It's a widening circle.

So, you expose ours and then someone will get interested and she tells someone else whose interested. So, we're not going to sell it! It's going to live up there forever.

That the Martha's Vineyard Preservation Trust would ever dispose of their historic merry-go-round is not a concern. Having acquired the Flying Horses to protect them, former Executive Director Jane Chittick's answer to the possibility of the Trustees of the Preservation Trust selling the horses was emphatic.

They never would! Preservation is in our title and that's our goal, to preserve a working full authentic carousel. Really to have it working and preserved both at the same time, not just preserved. That's one of the reasons we were chosen as a National Historic Landmark. They would not consider carousels that were placed in a museum like the Indianapolis Children's Museum. They would not consider that because its original intent was a source of amusement. That's what a carousel is. So, how can you not use it? It takes away it's spirit of movement if it's just preserved to look at.

Of course, the biggest problem and fear that I have — because we are open when we are open seven days a week, twelve hours a day — and being the most popular event on the Island, my fear is the machinery, being such an antique, breaking. The band organ breaking, and so forth. I have a small crew of people who know the carousel inside and out, who are dedicated to it. If something happens, they are there immediately fixing it. But, I think that is the biggest danger, because we believe that merry-go-rounds or carousels are to be operated, not simply looked at or stared at as a museum piece.

Before each ride, the operators give the safety instructions, fasten your belt, don't lean over, this sort of stuff. They start out saying this is the oldest carousel in America, built in 1876, and purchased by the Preservation Trust. They give a brief history of it and that is done when every ride begins. We feel very strongly that people know what it is.

Everyone knows the carousel and it's right in the heart of Oak Bluffs. That building is actually the original building dating from 1884. The building and carousel itself were moved in 1896 to the location which you see now. The building itself is also a National Historic Landmark in addition to the carousel.

Everyone felt strongly about the carousel. The support was overwhelming, really. The number of people who were not supportive you could count on your hand. I think it just conjured up their past, their memories. I mean, there have been generations who have ridden these horses. They even go back to their grandparents.

We had donations from almost every state in the country and some abroad because many people come to the Vineyard and live elsewhere. And everyone rides the Flying Horses carousel. It's part of their memories as a child. We had letters from people who were well into their eighties who reminisced about the first time that they rode on a carousel. There was this terribly huge popular support.

Besides its historical importance, it really gives such a great deal of joy to everyone who is there, whether they're riding the carousel or looking on. It's just a very happy place. It's one place people go in — they've fought traffic and crowds outside in the street — they step in here and it is pure delight and joy. We have lots of people who just go in to watch others have fun. As many onlookers as riders.

At the end of the year, we put a lot of money back into the building and the carousel. Unlike maybe what other owners would do, because, of course, that's our mission.

For the most part, carousels owned by municipalities, such as the Broome County merry-go-rounds, are not in danger of being broken up and sold at auction. Other carousels that have a good chance of future survival are those still in storage and not yet part of the contemporary scene. Carousels belonging to two of the narrators fall into this category. About his carousel, Charles Walker states:

I'm currently looking around at several possibilities of places to put it together because the developers are still of the mind that they want to put something on this block and we're the only hold out on the block. The reason being the merry-go-round is not finished, so the merry-go-round is holding up progress in a way. But what has to happen is a spot needs to be decided on and that's a very tricky problem. You want to be somewhere where there's not a whole lot of civil disobedience and you want to be someplace where you know that for a few years it's going to be stable. That's difficult in this day and town to discover.

You sort of have a choice in this business of whether to have it in a metropolitan area and put up with the guff that goes with that. If you could buy a space and build a building that would be suitable, that would be the ideal situation and you would have control over it. The other thing is to be in a touristy area and close down in the winter months.

Six Flags tried to buy this one when they got the big beautiful one that they have out there, which is probably one of the finest carousels in the country. Or lease it to an amusement park. There are several. That's a thought. I figure that the little carousel that I have, I should be able to test the water with that. Then when I get ready to build a two-hundred-fifty thousand dollar building or whatever it takes to put this thing in. . . . It's kinda like sitting on an oil well and you'd like to run a little hose down and sort of lubricate the machinery, except if you do the whole thing falls in, so it's kind of hard to know. This summer I'm going to do some more looking and see if I can discover that perfect place or something that's reasonable.

I hope that there'll still be some carousels out there in future years. And children will be able to have the grand thrill of being able to ride the wonderful old machines. If you have a carousel involved with a museum situation, then the children have something to relate to. They can go there and have fun at the museum, which is building an audience for the museum. Out in St. Louis, you've got a museum that has a carousel in it. We need to know that carousels need to be other places besides amusement parks. City parks. Museums. It's inexpensive entertainment, where you don't have to pay big piles of money to go to a theme park. You can go

Figure 107. Mario Coumo, Ex-Governor of New York State, takes a ride on the carousel at Recreation Park, Binghamton, New York. (Photo: Ed Aswad, Carriage House Photography)

and pay a dollar or fifty cents or seventy-five cents for a ride on a carousel, and it's just like having a little piece of candy.

I feel that as long as I have this carousel that it is safe. It won't go anywhere. And, there are a lot of them out there that are not safe. That's what I'm busy trying to work on.

Charlotte Dinger agrees that locating carousels in a museum setting is an ideal way to save endangered merry-go-rounds.

I like very much to see wooden carousels in museums because I know they're going to be taken care of properly. There are a number of them in museums today that are operating. There's one at Heritage Plantation in Massachusetts. The Indianapolis Children's Museum has one, and there's one going into a museum in Lansing, Michigan soon that came from Barnesville, Pennsylvania. So there is that trend.

And also, the major parks like Knotts Berry Farm, Disney, and Six Flags, all have antique carousels. They have the money and wherewithal to preserve them, and that's fine. I think that's going to be the future of the carousel. It's either going to be in a museum or in one of the major theme parks.

I have two carousel frames in storage, and I hope someday to put one of them back into operation. If it's in the right spot and if it's properly maintained and supervised, I would love to do that. I have a very lovely Dentzel frame. It's very ornate, and, of course, I'd put animals from my collection on the carousel. It would be very grand. But it just has to be in the right place. I would love to see it stay in New Jersey. That would be wonderful.

I also have a collection of animated circus miniatures that came from the Circus World Museum in Florida that are just spectacular. I'd like to put together a museum that would house the circus miniatures, as well as the carousel animals, even though circus and carousel are not really related.

It would have to be in an area where there's a lot of traffic, which would be sensible. In an art center would be lovely. Asbury Park if that ever revitalizes or Atlantic City. Anyplace that had to do, years ago, with carousels and amusements. Someplace where there are a lot of people, but yet a very nice place.

The carousel I have in storage would have really grand animals. Oh, I would love to see it in the green in Morristown. Right in the center of the green in a very lovely building.

The New England Carousel Museum in Bristol, Connecticut, already is a successful reality. As William Finkelstein reports:

The museum is a separate entity now. We bought it in February and we moved in and opened to the public in May, 1989. That's how quick it was. And, we realized we couldn't be a captain of three ships and do it well. We were pulling ourselves in all different directions. My wife was doing the gift shop. I was doing the museum and the restoration company along with her. It was just so much. We said, "We want to see it go on. We want to see it go on beyond us." Maybe it's taken a lot of effort, but it still means more if it can go on. So we said, "How can we do this?" Well, we'll let it go non-profit. We'll put a board in place and let them keep this for future generations. And that's what we did. The museum became non-profit.

There's magic in these pieces. It doesn't make any difference if you're ninety-nine or two years old, when you come through this door you're young again. It's a part of that whole thing. So, our motto became, *"Let The Magic Touch The Child In You."* I just pray that we can continue doing what we do because, I think, it does bring a positive note, a smile to people's faces so that's good. It brings joy to people.

Figure 108. Marcus Illions horses from the Pleasure Beach carousel in Bridgeport, Connecticut, now on display at the New England Carousel Museum in Bristol Connecticut. (Photo: Kate Langeway)

Figure 109. This stylized "rose" Parker horse is a favorite among visitors to the New England Carousel Museum. (Photo: Kate Langeway)

The popularity of the carousel has led to a revival of the art of wood carving, particularly the carving of miniature merry-go-rounds. George Long of Seabreeze Park in Rochester carved some five hundred miniature figures before his death. Carousel animal carving kits with small through full size figures are available for the new carver. The Herschell Carousel Factory Museum in North Tonawanda, New York, offers a summer carving program where one takes home a finished product. Many carvers today are doing full size figures for their own pleasure or for sale. Using the traditional hand methods of the original master carvers, Gerry Holzman and other New York carvers continue to work on the Empire State Carousel. Gerry Holzman says:

> We crossed the line two or three years ago. I call it the line from *if* to *when*. People used to say, "If it's done, when will it be?" Now they say, "When it's done, where will it be?" So it's a very real thing. There's a line in *Tucker*, the movie about Tucker designing the car, and there's a moment in there where one of the fellows whose helping him says, "Never get too close to a dreamer because you'll catch his dream."

And this is what's happened. We just have an awful lot of support, just so many people.

Our plans at this point — we're on a small lake here — we'd like to build an old Victorian roundhouse on that lake and put the carousel there from January through May. Then, when the weather breaks, we'd like to take it around and travel around the state with it for four or five months. It's going to be like the *Flying Dutchman*. It will travel forever.

Figure 110. The facade of the Empire State Carousel band organ shows New York state musicians George M. Cohan, John Philip Sousa and Irving Berlin. The decorative elements are derived from New York State fruits and vegetables. (Photo: Gerry Holzman)

We're developing exhibits now. We're thinking of making this a little traveling museum as well. A museum that would be a museum of New York state carousel history. So, what we hope to do — again still in the planning stage — is have traveling with us a large van, a walk in van which would show the history of the carousels of New York. Anybody familiar with the carousel knows that New York state, between Tonawanda and Brooklyn, produced probably forty percent of all the carousels made in America. We want to show the people. In short, what we're going to have is when we come to a location, a carousel will be set up which will be abso-

242

lutely unique. And, alongside it, will be set up peripheral exhibits which will tell the story of the carousel in New York.

Even though we have lost many wonderful carousels, the growing awareness of the hand-carved wooden merry-go-round as a national artistic and historical treasure hopefully will aid in the survival of those still in existence. Others now in storage or undergoing restoration will come back on the scene. And brand new traditionally carved carousels will make their appearance.

In addition to these there will be an increase in modern fiberglass carousels. Importer of Italian carousels, Bernd Rennebeck contends that even fiberglass figures must be considered an art form because:

> You have to make a mold. You have to make an original [hand carved horse]. We could make copies of American horses, but I think the type of horse we use now fits very well with the general style [of the carousel].

> I like any of the ornate, old horses, but I don't like some of the angry looking ones. Some of them are really very angry looking. That's one of the reasons why we modified the horses we use on our carousels now. They are all gentle looking creatures. These Lippizan stallions are nice looking, almost smiling horses. All white with colorful trappings on them, except for one black horse that symbolizes good luck.

> Everything is hand painted on there. Each scenery panel is an original oil painting. It's not mass produced. The double decker carousels are from Italy. They are copies of the first double decker carousel made in Germany in 1898. A carpenter with his family [Phillip Schneider] made that for himself to travel with it. There are at least twenty-five of them here. We own fourteen of them.

> We own them and put them in shopping centers. In malls. That's where we operate them. Some malls were very interested in the carousel and the double decker because it creates the excitement and news coverage and all the things that malls want to bring people in. But they don't have the room, so we started also importing single decker, regular carousels that are styled the same. They just don't have the upper deck.

Figure 111. The horses and scenery panels on the upper and lower facades of the Venetian carousels imported by Bernd Rennbeck are all hand painted by Italian artists. The one black horse among the white Lippizan-style stallions on the carousel is an Italian symbol of good luck. (Photo: Courtesy Bernd Rennebeck)

We did several tests where the mall developer was not one hundred percent convinced that it would be a good thing for the mall. They said, "Well, we'll go in on a trial basis." So, we'll go in on a thirty day lease. We haven't left anywhere yet!

We have imported fifty or sixty of them over the past ten years.

It seems that carousels are not going to disappear as long as we have today's "Carousel Keepers" to protect them. They may not be the favorite merry-go-rounds that we remember from childhood, and they may not be located in the home town park, but for today's children they will hold the same enchantment. Whether found in one of the great theme parks or the local mall, the magic of the carousel will endure to carry future generations back to a gentler time when long summer days were lived at a slower, calmer pace.

Bibliography

Abbate, James E. *National Amusement Park Historical News*, Vol. 2, No. 1, Jan.-Feb. 1980.

_____ *National Amusement Park Historical News*, Vol. 3, No. 3, May-June 1981.

_____ *National Amusement Park Historical News*, Vol. 8, No's. 4 & 5, 1986.

_____ *National Amusement Park Historical News*, Vol. 9, No. 4, 1987.

_____ *National Amusement Park Historical News*, Vol. 11, No. 5, 1989.

_____ *National Amusement Park Historical News*, Vol. 12, No. 3, 1990.

Barach, Kathleen. *The Last Carousel, City Park, New Orleans*, New Orleans: Friends of City Park, 1991.

Dinger, Charlotte. *Art of the Carousel*, Green Village, NJ: Carousel Art Inc., 1983.

Griffen, Al. *"Step Right Up Folks!"* Chicago, IL: Henry Regnery Company, 1974.

Fraley, Nina. *The American Carousel*, Benecia, CA: Redbug Workshop, 1979.

Fraley, Tobin. *The Carousel Animal*, Berkeley, CA: Zephyr Press, 1983.

Fried, Fred. *A Pictorial History of the Carousel*, Vestal, NY: Vestal Press, Ltd., 1964.

_____ "Last Ride for Carousel Figures?," *Historic Preservation*, Vol. 29 (July-Sept, 1977), pp. 22–27.

Herschell-Spillman Company, *Herschell-Spillman Company Catalog "G,"* Vestal, NY: Report by Vestal Press, Ltd., n.d.

Hinds, Anne Dion. *Grab the Brass Ring*, New York, NY: Crown Publishers Inc., 1990.

Hunter, Susan. *A Family Guide to Amusement Centers*, New York, NY: Walker & Company, 1975.

Manns, William, Peggy Shank and Marianne Stevens. *Painted Ponies*, Millwood, NY: Zon International Publishing Company, 1986.

Onosko, Tim. *Funland, U.S.A. The Complete Guide to 100 Major Amusement and Theme Parks*, New York, NY: Ballantine Books, 1978.

Paschen, Stephen H., *Shootin the Chutes*, Akron, OH: Summit County Historical Society, 1988.

Philadelphia Toboggan Company, *The Seabreeze Park Carousel and Selected Pictures of Philadelphia Toboggan Company Carrousels As Taken from Early Catalog Material*, Vestal, NY: Vestal Press, Ltd., n.d.

Ulmer, Jeff. *Amusement Parks of America, A Comprehensive Guide*, New York: The Dial Press, 1980.

Walker, Charles, *The Carousel is the Greatest Show in Town*, Atlanta, GA: National Carousel Association, n.d.

_____*The Carousel is the Ticket to a Successful Amusement Business*, Atlanta, GA: National Carousel Association, n.d.

_____*Safe Tips on Carousel Operation*, Atlanta, GA: National Carousel Association. n.d.

_____*An Alternative to the Auctioneers Block*, Atlanta, GA: National Carousel Association. n.d.

_____*The Road Carousel, the Pride of the Midway*, Atlanta, GA: National Carousel Association. n.d.

_____*Avoiding the Unpredictible Breakdown*, Atlanta, GA: National Carousel Association. n.d.

_____*The Squeak Gets the Grease*, Atlanta, GA: National Carousel Association, n.d.

For additional information on carousels see all issues of the following:

The Merry-go-Roundup, a quarterly publication of The National Carousel Association, Cynthia L. Hennig, Editor, 620 Park Avenue, #311, Rochester, NY 14607

The Carousel News & Trader, a monthly magazine published by The Carousel News & Trader, 87 Park Avenue West, Suite 206, Mansfield, OH 44902

Index